The Motley Crew

The Motley Crew
Monastic Lives

Brother Benet Tvedten

LITURGICAL PRESS
Collegeville, Minnesota

www.litpress.org

271.0092(2)
TVM

Cover design by David Manahan, O.S.B. Illustration: St. Benedict and
St. Scholastica at Sacro Speco, Subiaco. 15th century fresco painting.

1	2	3	4	5	6	7	8

Library of Congress Cataloging-in-Publication Data

Tvedten, Benet.
    The motley crew : monastic lives / Benet Tvedten.
        p.   cm.
    ISBN-13: 978-0-8146-3177-5
    ISBN-10: 0-8146-3177-0
    1. Monasticism and religious orders—Biography.   I. Title.

BX2800.T88 2007
271.0092'2—dc22
[B]

2006017278

Contents

Introduction:
We Are a Motley Crew

St. Bernard of Clairvaux, a great medieval abbot, claimed that a monk achieved greater purity than other people and sinned less frequently. On the other hand, he often spoke and wrote in a more realistic frame of mind, describing monks who lived a great distance from perfection and who were responsible for causing chaos in their monasteries. Some were braggarts who craved recognition for their accomplishments. Others boasted of sins committed before coming to the monastery, and some even boasted of indecent things they'd done since becoming monks. There were also monks who were so puffed up by self-importance that they refused to perform certain menial tasks in the monastery.

When I entered the abbey almost fifty years ago, monasticism was still called "the state of perfection." The church applied this misleading label, and we no longer use it. In some instances, persons from outside the monastery have revealed our grave sins as well as our imperfections. England's late Cardinal Hume, while he was still the Abbot of Ampleforth, told young men who were being invested as novices that they were "joining a community composed of extremely imperfect human beings. You are not entering a community of saints. If that is what you thought we were, then please go before I clothe you. No, we are very human and it is important to remember this."

We are not saints. Nor have we all come out of the same mold. Once when Abbot Alan was preaching on the Feast of St. Benedict, he looked at us, his community of monks, and remarked, "If our Holy Father, the Patriarch of Monks, were here with us today, he would think we're a motley crew." This book offers thumbnail sketches of monastic ancestors and brief accounts of my own monastic journey through life. It begins where Benedictine monasticism began, giving portraits of important figures who lived in the desert and Europe. The second section gives an account of a time when our history was most threatened, during the Reformation. Benedictine monasticism did not, of course, end in the sixteenth century; it continued to rise and fall in Europe, and faced a resurgence at the time it moved to the New World. In the third section I follow our history in the United States, giving some portraits of important figures and our way of life as we continue to live the Rule. Some things stay the same, you will see. We always struggle to balance the contemplative and apostolic part of our mission. Personalities can sometimes dominate. In our long history we've seen over and over that wealth can be the biggest threat to keeping the discipline of the Rule. Still, ours is a joyful and somewhat messy history, not unlike the history of all people striving to draw closer to God.

The Motley Crew

The Father of Monasticism

St. Benedict did not invent monasticism in the sixth century. It, along with prostitution, is one of the oldest professions around. Monasticism is common not just to Christianity, but is found in many of the world's religions. The beginnings of Christian monasticism can be traced to Egypt with the hermit St. Antony, the Patriarch of Monasticism in the East.

Antony was born in 251. Although his father was a wealthy landowner, the son was uneducated. From childhood he refused to attend school because he did not want to associate with other children. He was already a hermit. In late adolescence, both of his parents died, and Antony was left in charge of their property and his young sister.

One day on his way to Mass, he was recalling how the Christians in *Acts* sold their property and gave the money to the poor. When he arrived at church late, the gospel was being read. Antony heard our Lord's admonition to sell your property, give the money to the poor, and then come follow him. So, he gave away all three hundred acres of his property and sold the other possessions, giving most of the proceeds to the poor. He kept back some for the benefit of his sister. Then the word of the Lord spoke to him again in church about not being anxious regarding the future. This time Antony gave away his sister. He placed her in a convent and went off to embrace the ascetical life.

There were other ascetics living in the neighborhood, and he received his instructions from them. After learning how to be a hermit, Antony found his own place of solitude. The devil, how-ever, was watching and tried discouraging him by suggesting that he should really repossess all that property. Then he riddled the hermit with guilt for having abandoned his little sister. But Antony persevered. The devil tried again by running a lot of X-rated movies through Antony's mind. The young hermit blushed but remained faithful to his calling. Accustomed to the ascetical life now, Antony moved farther away from his native village. Out in the desert he found a tomb. Arranging to have bread brought to him now and then, he had himself sealed up in the tomb. The devil got in, though, and attacked Antony physically, beating him into unconsciousness. When the hermit revived, he told the devil to go back to hell. The devil attempted scaring him into submission. Demons arrived in the tomb hermitage at night and made a terrible racket. Wild beasts got in and reptiles more numerous than those in the movie where Indiana Jones fell into a serpent's pit.

Nowadays, we would say that he was hallucinating because of his improper diet and lack of sleep. For Antony and other desert monks, fasting and keeping vigil were the norms of reli-gious observance, and encountering the devil was a common experience. The devil had no use for people who wanted to discipline their lives. St. Benedict, in the first chapter of his Rule, describes various kinds of monks. Of anchorites or hermits, he says, "they are now trained to fight against the devil" (*RB* 1.4). This training was received by living in community initially, but when the hermit left the community he had to keep in training for "the single combat of the desert" (*RB* 1.5). We all know how difficult it is to discipline ourselves. In order to entice me into abandoning my Lenten fast, the devil doesn't have to lock me up in a cage with wild animals. The abbey baker can accomplish my downfall by serving cream puffs on Ash Wednesday.

Antony and the devil were in conflict for many years. The time came when they were able to converse in a civilized man-ner. Antony admitted that he was a fool for even discussing the ascetical life with the devil. The devil confessed that his job on earth had become more difficult because of the Redeemer's appearance on the scene. He had observed that there were Christians everywhere, and now even the desert was overcrowded with Christian ascetics. Antony asked him if he was ready to cry uncle. The devil said he was.

At the age of thirty-five, Antony left the tomb, looking for a more remote place. Coming across a deserted fort, he made it his new hermitage and lived there for twenty years. Some aspirants to the ascetical life wanted him to be their guru, and they broke down the door to the fort. Antony emerged and everyone was surprised to see what fine shape he was in. He was not overweight from lack of exercise, nor was he emaciated from fasting.

Antony became the *Abba* (Father) of many ascetics, other solitaries whose cells were near his so that they could go to him for instruction. Twice he left his hermitage for trips to Alexandria, once to comfort Christians who were imprisoned during a persecution, and again to confront Arians who were denying the divinity of Christ. He never saw his sister again, but he learned that she had grown old and had become the Mother (*Amma*) of her community.

Antony grew old too, very old. At the approach of his death, he instructed two of his disciples to take the contents of his wardrobe for themselves: two skins, a cloak, and a camel's hair hood. He was 105—without a wrinkle on his face, and with all of his teeth.

St. Benedict, while acknowledging the validity of the hermetical life with all its rigors, chose to legislate for cenobitical monks—those who live in a monastery. Living under an abbot and with other monks is penance enough.

The Father of Cenobitical Monasticism

*P*achomius is the Eastern monk recognized as the Father of Cenobitical Monasticism. He was an Egyptian who was drafted into the Roman army at the age of twenty. On their way to camp, the draftees were kept overnight in a jail so they wouldn't escape from military duty. There were some Christians being held there simply because of their religion. Pachomius was impressed by them. He resolved to serve their God upon his release from the army.

In 315, he came across a deserted village called Tabennesis, and this became his monastic foundation. Seven thousand monks entered the community during his lifetime, and Pachomius wrote a rule for them. His sister became the abbess of a women's monastery at Tabennesis.

Some former hermits found it difficult living in community. Gripers of any kind were reprimanded up to five times. If a monk didn't change his attitude after that, Pachomius sent him to the infirmary as a sick man.

Pachomius, however, once had a legitimate gripe about his monks. In the beginning of their monastic life, the monks worked on farms in the area. Pachomius brought these field hands their lunch. As the monks increased in numbers, Pachomius had to procure an ass to take him around to the farms. Now and then a monk would climb on the animal and ride back to the monastery, leaving Pachomius to return on foot, carrying all the eating utensils.

An angel is reputed to have written the first part of Pachomius' Rule. When he complained there were too few prayers, the angel replied that it was arranged this way so that the weaker members would be able to keep the rule and not "grieve." St. Benedict will be of the same mind when he says there should be no reason for "justifiable grumbling" in the monastery.

In reality, monks have never given up the practice of complaining. At our monthly Chapter of Faults, some monks will usually confess to griping about things in general or in particular. Whatever its cause, the grumbling is not justifiable.

Basil the Great

*I*n the same century as St. Pachomius, there was another monastic legislator named Basil. He was born in Caesarea (modern Turkey). Basil's grandmother, his parents, sister, two younger brothers, and himself are all venerated as saints in the Eastern Church.

While studying in the schools of Constantinople and Athens, Basil's sister, Macrina, and their widowed mother turned the family home into a monastery. Basil was attracted to the ascetical life, but not as a hermit, and he thought the size of Pachomian monasticism would make life unbearable for him. With a good friend, Gregory of Nazianzus, he began monastic life in a place that the latter found unsuitable. The house was too small, its roof leaked, the stream that flowed by had few fish but lots of rocks, and the garden couldn't produce beans. Here was another monastic griper. Gregory, however, chose to leave.

He went home to Nazianzus, and was ordained by his father who was the bishop there. Gregory became the bishop of a place where Arianism was rife. He was instrumental in suppressing the heresy. Years later, the Emperor Theodosius made him the Archbishop of Constantinople. Gregory resigned soon after, in the midst of controversy, and went to live in seclusion. We presume the roof of his house did not leak and that he was able to grow beans in his garden.

Basil's Long Rules and Short Rules are statements on monastic life in the form of questions and answers. There was no formal novitiate, but commitment was permanent. One could be dispensed, presumably for reasons more serious than Gregory's. A married man was accepted into Basil's monastery if he had received his wife's permission. Freed slaves were made welcome and escaped ones if their masters had been cruel. The monks prayed the psalms, studied Scripture, and worked with their hands and with their heads. They taught school and operated hospitals.

In contrasting their life with the hermetical, Basil referred to our Lord's washing of the apostles' feet, and asked the hermits whose feet they would wash. Basil, while still a monastic superior, was named Bishop of Caesarea. He is the prototype monk-bishop. Other monks in both the East and the West were made bishops throughout history and still are today.

North African Voice

*I*n this pre-Benedictine era of monasticism, there is another legislator of a rule. We tend to remember St. Augustine mostly for his *Confessions*. His mother, Monica, died as she and her son were returning to their home in Northern Africa after years of living in Rome. Augustine, now fully converted to Christianity, intended to start a monastery on family property in Thagaste. He was joined by his friend, Alypius. Like Basil, Augustine started out with a friend. He had known Alypius in Milan. The two of them, along with mutual friends, had started a commune of sorts in Milan. It did not last because the girlfriends of the ten men objected.

Augustine was also accompanied to Thagaste by his son, fathered with the woman who'd been his mistress for twelve years. The youth was named Adeodatus, meaning "gift of God." When the boy died in 389, Augustine was bewildered and sad. He left Thagaste and resumed monastic life in Hippo, where he, like Basil, eventually became a bishop.

Augustine addressed himself to many monastic issues. One of his works dealt with the length of monks' hair. He asked if men those days were trying to provide more leisure for barbers or if, like birds, they were afraid of not being able to fly if their plumage was plucked. He advised monks not "to be influenced by the foolish arguments of the vain and not to imitate in perversity those to whom, in other respects, they are so unlike." I was conducting a retreat at a monastery where a prospective candidate was looking it over. One of the monks indicated to me that if the young man was accepted into their novitiate, "That pony tail will have to go." On the other hand, we have a monk in our community whom none of us has ever seen without his pony tail.

The Rule of St. Augustine was adopted by many religious congregations down through the ages. The Order that bears his name was founded in the thirteenth century.

Abbot Benedict Himself

St. Benedict is called the Patriarch of Monasticism in the West. He had a great respect for the monastic teachings of the East. These were compiled by John Cassian (+435), and Benedict refers to them in the last chapter of his Rule, along with his praise for St. Basil. "Besides the *Conferences* of the Fathers, their *Institutes* and their *Lives,* there is also the rule of our holy Father Basil" (*RB* 73.5). Benedict, comparing the monks of his day with those of old, says that the former practices "make us blush for shame at being so slothful, so unobservant, so negligent" (*RB* 73.7).

Some people may have thought of monks and nuns—living in their "state of perfection"—as the holiest of the holy. St. Benedict knew how difficult monastic life could be. I'm thinking of the many obstacles he had to overcome. In the beginning, he had to suppress lustful temptations of youth. He had to face two assassination attempts: one by his monks and the other by a priest from the neighborhood. There were accidents in the construction of his monastery at Monte Cassino. He put up with clumsy, careless monks, monks who disobeyed, and monks who lied. Living in a monastery is enough to try the patience of any saint. In chapter 72 of the Rule, Benedict says monks are to support "with the greatest patience one another's weaknesses of body or behavior" (*RB* 72.5). The abbot is also instructed to be mindful of his own frailties. The Rule of St. Benedict was clearly written for people who were not yet holy.

St. Benedict drew upon a monastic rule written by someone known only as The Master. In 1937, a French monastic scholar reported that this was the case, but it took a long while for the whole Benedictine world to accept this fact. The first English translation of the Rule of the Master was published in 1971. Reading it and making the comparison, it is obvious what Benedict kept, what he discarded, and what is original. The Master's Rule has far too many details. It is tedious and repetitious. The Master creates a lot of fuss over trivial matters, and he is overly suspicious of monks and guests, even a clerical or monastic one. For example: Two monks are assigned to sleep in the same room as a guest. The door is locked and one of the monks keeps the key. If the guest must rise in the night to answer nature's call, one of the monks must accompany him to make sure that the guest doesn't steal anything on his way to the latrine and back. Benedict sets the tone for hospitality by merely stating that all guests at the monastery are to be received as Christ.

At vespers on the Solemnity of St. Benedict, we sing a hymn in which the second verse refers to our Holy Father Benedict living in heaven while on earth. Ha! St. Benedict did not live with his head in the clouds. Although a monastery might be called "a heavenly place" by those who don't live in one, the inhabitants know that it isn't the dwelling place of angels. Benedict knew his monastery was rooted here on earth. A monastery is the place from which we take off for heaven, but no monk or nun ever got there already canonized. Benedict says, "The reason we have written this rule is that, by observing it in monasteries, we can show that we have some degree of virtue and the beginnings of monastic life" (*RB* 73.1). He counts himself among those who are seeking virtue, but who have not yet reached perfection. Benedictines are like members of Alcoholics Anonymous. Here is what they say about their program of recovery: "No one among us has been able to maintain anything like perfect adherence to these principles. We are not saints. The point is that we are willing to grow along spiritual lines. We claim spiritual progress rather than spiritual perfection." It is often necessary for monks to admit they are imperfect and to ask forgiveness. Although our sins are personal, some of them offend the society in which we live.

Benedict tells us not to give up on ourselves. The conclusion of the Prologue to his Rule holds out hope. "As we progress in this way of life and in faith, we shall run on the path of God's commandments, our hearts overflowing with the inexpressible delight of love. Never swerving from his instructions, then, but faithfully observing his teaching in the monastery until death, we shall through patience share in the sufferings of Christ that we may deserve also to share in his kingdom" (*RB* Pro. 49-50).

Scholastica

$\mathcal{B}$enedict had a sister named Scholastica. She is mentioned only once in the biography of her brother. He spent the day with her at a house owned by his monastery. After the evening meal, they continued visiting until Benedict realized he shouldn't be absent from his community any longer. She pleaded with him to stay overnight, but he insisted that it was impossible for him to do so. Scholastica prayed up so severe a storm that Benedict couldn't even think of leaving. He complained "bitterly," the biographer reports.

Three days later, Benedict saw the soul of his sister ascending to heaven in the form of a dove. "Overjoyed at her eternal glory, he gave thanks to God in hymns of praise. Then, after informing his brethren of her death, he sent some of them to bring her body to the abbey and bury it in the tomb he had prepared for himself." He must surely have admitted to himself how foolish he'd been the last time he saw her alive.

In their last encounter on this earth, Benedict had acted contrary to his nature. He is the man who had instructed his monks to never turn away from anyone who needed their love. And now here he is refusing a simple request from his sister. She only wants him to pray with her and to continue their discourse on heavenly subjects. Indignantly, he tells her that he cannot be away from his monastery. The law is the law. Besides, some of Benedict's monks came along with him, and he would be showing them a bad example by submitting to Scholastica's request. Chapter 42 of his Rule begins: "Monks should diligently cultivate silence at all times, but especially at night." He will not soften the discipline, not even for the sake of a sibling. He'll not stay up all night talking with her. She should have better sense than to ask him to break night silence. Benedict will attempt turning away from Scholastica in this hour of her need. The narrator of the story asks, "Do we not read in St. John that God is love? Surely it is no more than right that her influence was greater than his, since hers was the greatest love." She taught her brother that the law might be bent for the sake of love. Benedict is reminded that in drawing up his regulations, he hoped "to set down nothing harsh, nothing burdensome" (*RB* Pro. 46).

Scholastica has been traditionally called Benedict's twin, but some scholars tell us twinning was a medieval literary practice. For that matter, so was the creation of a sister in the biography of a male saint. Was Scholastica a nun or did she live piously in her own home with a private vow of celibacy? Scholars debate this too. For that matter, they also question her very existence. At Monte Cassino, though, the inscription on the tomb reads: "This single tomb holds them both—born together and in their lives one in holiness."

Paul the Deacon, an eighth-century monk of Monte Cassino, relates how some Franks came to the abbey, pretending to keep vigil at this tomb. Instead, they stole the remains of the saints from right under the eyes of the monks. Paul says the French may have the bones, but the dust to which Benedict and Scholastica have returned still remains at Monte Cassino. The bones were enshrined at the monastery of Fleury. A German monk, writing about the thievery, observed that when Benedict and Scholastica rose again on the last day, they would do so on French soil. But the monks of Monte Cassino asked Pope Zachary to intercede for them, and the precious relics were returned to Italy in 757.

Irish Monasticism

Ireland was never part of the Roman Empire. Therefore it was not Romanized when it became Christian. The Irish insisted on being an indigenous church, much to the annoyance of the inhabitants of the neighboring island who wanted to be recognized as Roman Christians.

Once I had occasion to witness the ruins at Clonmacnois, founded by St. Ciaran in the sixth century. For a thousand years, students from Ireland and abroad attended the schools established in this monastic city situated on the banks of the River Shannon. The water route made it convenient for them to get to school, and it provided access to Viking ships as well. The ruins of the monks' and nuns' churches and the Round Towers in which they hid from their Scandinavian plunderers are now tourist attractions. Three fine examples of Irish high crosses with biblical scenes carved into the stones are also preserved at Clonmacnois.

Father Laurence, an Irish monk who brought me to the site, pointed to a circular platform in an open area, and asked if I could name that particular monastic artifact. I suggested that it was something modern. "It's made of concrete." He laughed. This was the landing pad for the papal helicopter on the day John Paul II came to Clonmacnois.

When the Irish were converted to Christianity, they took to monasticism like no other people in the world have. They were clannish and so was their monasticism. Monks and nuns formed communities along clan lines. A monastery was the ideal place for sons of a clan who were not eligible for inheriting farmland, and for daughters who couldn't find husbands.

The Irish obsession with penance was another attractive aspect of monastic life. Irish monks confessed their sins twice a day. This may seem unreasonable. How could anyone find that many sins to confess? The Irish did some investigation into the matter, and came up with a list of every imaginable sin a human being could commit. They called this list a penitential.

Columban was an Irish abbot who wrote a rule. He was born in 545, two years before Benedict's death. Even if Columban had known about the Rule of St. Benedict, he would have still preferred his own because it was more severe. He made monks who were ill work. Obedience was so prompt that a cellarer who was called by the abbot while filling a jug with beer hastened to him without turning off the spigot. To test his monks' obedience on another occasion, the abbot yelled, "Colman, jump in the lake." Twelve Colmans promptly obeyed the command.

Monks were punished for coughing at communal prayer—twelve strikes to the body. For smiling during prayer—six strikes. Allowance was made for laughter, however, if a humorous mistake had been made. Ah, the lilt of Irish laughter.

A woman hermit urged young Columban to join a monastery. His was not your typical Irish mother of yore who had been praying that the Lord might call a son of hers. She protested and pleaded and prostrated on the ground, but he stepped right over her, and went off to become a monk.

Not only did Columban leave his mother, he left Ireland too. The Irish monks were missionaries who wandered all over. The efforts of Irish missionary monks were not always appreciated by bishops who wanted to establish a church that adhered to Roman ways.

In Gaul, Columban founded monasteries without even asking permission from bishops. They opposed the liturgical practices of the Irish, and like the English, they abhorred the Irish celebration of Easter on a Sunday different from the one observed by the universal church. The bishops of Gaul didn't even like the way the Irish monks wore their hair. The Irish tonsure was over the head instead of around the head.

Gall, a disciple of Columban, went to Switzerland and established a monastery that later bore his name. The Abbey of St. Gall became one of the great monastic edifices of Europe when the Benedictines gained control of it. A number of Benedictine monasteries in France, Germany, and Italy were founded on sites where the Irish monks had been. The Irish were always on the move.

When complaints about Columban's orthodoxy were made to the pope, the Irish monk defended himself by claiming Irish respect for Rome ever since the time that Christ had come to their island borne on the back of a dolphin. That must have confused the pope. Such a statement by an Irish ecclesiastic points out another objection of the Romanists: there was more than a wee bit of Celtic myth mixed up with Irish Christianity.

Columban's Irish monasticism did not survive. It was replaced by Benedictinism, which had a more lasting effect because it was more stable and more humane.

Two Little Boys at School

Benedict called the monastery "a school for the Lord's service." We are given the names of two disciples of St. Benedict who entered this school as "very promising boys." Saints Maurus and Placid were brought to St. Benedict's monastery at Subiaco by their parents. When they grew up, Maurus supposedly went to Gaul to found a monastery, and Placid to Sicily, where he also founded a monastery, and was martyred. Historians, however, doubt that either of them went to the places where legend has assigned them.

The story told most often about the boys Maurus and Placid is how the former saved the latter from drowning. Placid had fallen into the lake when he went to fetch a bucket of water. Hearing the screaming boy, Abbot Benedict sent Maurus to rescue Placid. He ran to the lake and kept on running right over the water. "Pulling him up by the hair, Maurus rushed back to shore, still under the impression that he was on dry land." The lesson, of course, is what happens when obedience is promptly performed. On another occasion, Maurus disappointed Benedict. The disciple rejoiced at the death of the priest who had tried poisoning Benedict, and for this Maurus was given a penance to perform.

Benedict's biographer tells us that Maurus and Placid came from well-to-do families. When he wrote the Rule at Monte

Cassino, Benedict made it clear that boys offered to the monastery by rich parents were never to possess any of this wealth. In giving their sons to the monastery, Benedict offered these parents an annuity: "they may make a formal donation of the property that they want to give the monastery, keeping the revenue for themselves, should they so desire" (*RB* 59.5).

The sons of rich and poor were both given as a perpetual offering (an oblation). The parents presented their little boy to the monastery with his hands wrapped in the altar cloth. The Benedictine scholar, Terrence Kardong, says the ceremony described in The Rule is "as memorable as it is heartbreaking." Cardinal Newman's comments in *Historical Sketches* make it appear even more pitiable: "The little beings, of three or four or five years old, were brought in the arms of those who gave them life to accept at their bidding the course in which that life was to run." Newman, however, is praising the system. The practice of making an oblation of one's young son to a monastery was prohibited in later centuries, while the Benedictine tradition of educating the young continued.

The parents of St. Thomas Aquinas wanted him to become a monk at Monte Cassino, where he had gone to school as a boy. His family was not at all pleased when young Tom took up with a relatively new outfit called the Order of Preachers instead of joining the esteemed and ancient Order of St. Benedict. They had plans for him to advance to the abbacy of Monte Cassino. In such a position, he might be able to do something about restoring part of the property his family had lost. But he would never be able to do that if he became a wandering friar whose only ambition was to teach and preach against heresy. His relatives kidnapped him, and held him in their castle until he agreed to become a Benedictine monk. Thomas did not give in to their wishes, and they finally had to let him return to the religious order founded by a Spaniard named Dominic Guzman.

In his youth, Father Timothy Radcliffe, an English Dominican who served as the Master of the Order in recent years, attended two Benedictine schools: Worth and Downside. He remembers "the humanity of the monks, who helped me to believe in a God who was good and merciful, though very English!" Upon arriving at Worth, young Timothy and other new students were told they would be punished for every item of clothing dropped on the floor and left there at bedtime. He received six strikes of the cane his first night.

Benedict had a penchant for neatness and order. In chapter 30 of his Rule he says boys should be corrected "with sharp strokes so that they may be healed" (*RB* 30.3). A more recent translation reads that misbehaving boys should be "smacked." This seems to soften the punishment. Sadly enough, it has become evident that sexual and other kinds of abuse have occurred in Benedictine schools in modern times. Some people conclude that Benedict was guilty of enforcing physical abuse. A woman told me, "If he were living today, he'd be in prison." I'm confident that the manner in which he corrected boys was not severe enough to be considered physical abuse. In the case of young Timothy Radcliffe, the caning did not damage him. He learned to pick up his clothes as long as he was a student in a Benedictine school.

It's ironic that so many Benedictine men and women have run the kind of school from which Benedict himself dropped out. "He took this step, fully aware of his ignorance, yet he was truly wise, uneducated though he may have been," his biographer informs us. Abandoning the school in Rome where so many of his fellow students were more attuned to sinful pleasures than to study, Benedict founded a school for the Lord's service.

Over the centuries, many students of the Benedictines, now that they had a choice, stayed on and became monks or nuns. These schools imparted secular and religious wisdom. They were also centers for training in the arts and crafts. The Benedictines preserved learning and culture as Europe entered the Dark Ages.

Bede the Venerable

Bede is an English monastic saint who was placed in a monastery as a small boy. He provides an autobiographical note in his *History of the English Church and People:* "I was born on the lands of this monastery, and on reaching seven years of age, I was entrusted by my family first to the most reverend Abbot Benedict [Biscop] and later to Abbot Ceolfrid for my education. I have spent all the remainder of my life in this monastery and devoted myself entirely to the study of the Scriptures. And while I have observed the regular discipline and sung the choir offices daily in church, my chief delight has always been in study, teaching, and writing."

Perhaps Bede is best known as an historian—the first to date events *Anno Domini*. He was also a biographer, a Scripture exegete, a poet, a literary critic, a philosopher, and a theologian. He covered all the subjects that interested him. This included a book on orthography, the science of correct spelling. He composed hymns, compiled a martyrology, and edited a collection of homilies. The monks in the scriptorium were never at a loss for work while Bede was in their midst. He was also recognized as a reputable mathematician and astronomer. The man is called "the Venerable" because of his wisdom and learning.

Bede was born in the north of England in 672. Obviously, he never had any regrets about his parents having taken him to a monastery as a seven-year-old and leaving him there. When a plague attacked the monastery, the abbot and a boy oblate were the only ones left to pray the Divine Office. The boy was Bede. Abbot Ceolfrid decided that parts of the Divine Office should be shortened because of the choir's reduced circumstances, but after a week neither of them was satisfied with this arrangement. The full office was restored.

The monastic historian David Knowles summed up Bede's life this way: "It was an uneventful life and an undistinguished life: Bede never became a bishop, nor even an abbot, and he never met or influenced directly the rulers of Church or State. Even his undoubted holiness was unobtrusive. He wrote of the wonders worked by others, but none are recorded of him. He described the conversion of England, but he probably never preached to anyone outside his monastery."

Bede was ordained a deacon at the age of nineteen, but he did not become a priest until he was thirty. In the year 735 he died shortly after First Vespers of the Feast of the Ascension. Even to the very end of his life he was working on a manuscript—a translation of John's Gospel into English. He died after dictating the last sentence to the scribe at his bedside. His life is a model of the ordinariness of monastic life.

Whenever I read Cardinal Newman's words describing the monk, done in calligraphy, nicely framed, and hanging on a wall just outside our cloister, I think of Bede especially: "He went forth in his youth to work and to his labor until the evening of his life, if he lived a day longer, he did a day's work more; whether he lived many or few, he labored on to the end of them. He had no wish to see further in advance of his journey than where he was to mark his next stage. He ploughed and sowed, he prayed, he meditated, he studied, he wrote, he taught, and then he died and went to heaven."

The Pope and
the Archbishop of Canterbury

Although Pope St. Gregory and St. Augustine of Canterbury were both monks, they were not Benedictines. Our Father Gregory at Blue Cloud was always terribly annoyed whenever one of us reminded him that the saint who had been his heavenly patron for over fifty years had never been a member of our order.

"Blessed Gregory is a mirror for monks. He gave us the account of our Holy Father Benedict." This is an antiphon from the Divine Office for the Feast of St. Gregory. He was born in 540, sixty years after Benedict's birth. From the time I entered the novitiate and learned about my Benedictine forbearers, Pope St. Gregory the Great was presumed to have been St. Benedict's biographer. The *Life* had been written less than fifty years after Benedict's death, the scholars said. Now there is some doubt about Gregory's authorship and the date the biography was written. Perhaps one day there will be a consensus regarding what is now a controversy among the scholars.

Gregory was born in the city Benedict despised and from which he fled in his youth. Benedict scorned the schools of Rome; Gregory thrived in them. His educational background and his administrative abilities earned for him the position of prefect of Rome in 570. At the age of thirty-five, he turned his family home on the Coelian Hill into a monastery and became a monk. The daughters of Mother Teresa of Calcutta live on this site in present-day Rome. Gregory was called from his monastery to serve as papal nuncio in Constantinople for seven years. In 590, a reluctant Gregory was elected to the papacy. He would have preferred living out the rest of his days in the monastery. Being a pope instead of a monk took its toll on him. "Indeed when I was in the monastery I could curb my idle talk and usually be absorbed in my prayers. Since I assumed the burden of pastoral care, my mind can no longer be collected; it is concerned with so many matters. I am forced to consider the affairs of the Church and of the monasteries."

Pope Gregory, however, was not reluctant in taking another monk out of the monastery and sending him away from Rome. This was Augustine of Canterbury, not to be confused with the other Augustine who wrote his *Confessions*. Bede, in his *History of the English Church and People*, tells us everything we know about Augustine, who was as reluctant to be a missionary as Gregory was to be a pope. Once when Gregory was still prefect of Rome, he happened to see some young blond male captives. Inquiring about them, he was told they were Angles from Britain. Gregory said they looked more like angels. It was these people to whom Pope Gregory sent Augustine as a missionary in 597.

In the beginning Augustine and his monastic companions were unlikely models for missionaries. Bede says "they were appalled at the idea of going to a barbarous, fierce, and pagan nation, of whose very language they were ignorant." Nevertheless, they obeyed the Pope's command and left their monastery to go to a foreign land. But on the way, they began to count the cost, and asked to be recalled even before they were out of Italy. Gregory replied with words of encouragement. "So with the help of God you must carry out this holy task which you have begun." He also wrote to the Bishop of Arles in France where the forty monks would rest before setting sail for England. Gregory told the bishop to make "speedy provision for their needs." In other words, don't let them linger with you too long.

They arrived on the Isle of Thanet, off the coast of Kent, where they met King Ethelbert, and informed him of their mission. He replied that he had heard of Christianity. In fact, his Frankish wife was a Christian. Ethelbert was polite, but he was unwilling to convert to a new religion. He promised Augustine and company that they would not be prevented from preaching to anyone else in the realm. Then the king took them to the mainland and let them settle at a place called Canterbury. The mission was a success. Thousands of people were converted to Christianity, and King Ethelbert himself was eventually baptized.

Bede includes in his history the correspondence between Augustine and Gregory. The monk had never before been faced with the kinds of problems he encountered in the missionary field, and he depended on Pope Gregory for solutions. No longer was Augustine simply a monk laboring as a missionary; he had been consecrated the first Archbishop of Canterbury. He wanted to know what his relationship was to the clergy, how finances were to be distributed, and what exactly his duties were—all the things he need not have worried about when he was living in the monastery back in Rome. Gregory reminded Augustine that he was still a monk and so were all the clergy. Therefore, he must live with them under the monastic rule they all professed. If there were some monks who had not yet advanced to ordination, and who found celibacy a burden, Gregory recommended that they be released from their monastic vows. They were free to marry and still function as priests.

Augustine had many things on his mind. What should his relationship be with other bishops? How should people who have robbed churches be dealt with? Other questions pertained to marriage and sexual behavior. What degree of consanguinity was allowable in a marriage? Could a man come to church and receive communion immediately after having had sexual intercourse with his wife? Augustine told Pope Gregory, "These uncouth English people require guidance on all these matters." Gregory patiently responded to these questions. In a letter to King Ethelbert, Gregory told him, "Our most reverend brother Bishop Augustine has been trained under monastic rule, and has a complete knowledge of holy scripture, and by the grace of God, is a man of holy life." The monk Augustine knew Scripture, but it is evident from his questions to the pope that he was not versed in canon law or moral theology.

His travels through Europe on the way to England exposed Augustine to divergent practices in the church. This seems to have troubled him. Why, he wonders, can't the rest of the world adhere to the customs of Rome? Gregory respected indigenous culture. He advised Augustine to retain customs that were beneficial to the English people. Augustine had wanted to destroy their pagan temples, but Gregory told him to retain the buildings if they were of solid construction, and convert them into churches. Furthermore, he recommended diversity in religious observance. He said not everything had to be done in England as it was in Rome.

Today Augustine is recognized as the Apostle of England, but he might never have succeeded in his mission without the benevolent encouragement and prodding from the man in Rome. Bede, however, was willing to bestow the title of apostle on Gregory, giving him credit for bearing the responsibility of transforming "our still idolatrous nation into a church of Christ."

Hilda of Whitby

$\mathcal{B}$ ede, in his *History of the English Church and People*, wrote about Abbess Hilda of Whitby. She was born in Northumbria in 614, at a time when Christianity was still new in her country. Bishop Paulinus of York, one of the monks who had come from Rome with Augustine of Canterbury, baptized her when she was thirteen. Hilda's great-uncle, King Edwin of Northumbria, was baptized on the same day.

The Christianization of the English was not easily accomplished. Wars between the Christians and those tribes who refused to accept the new religion raged throughout the land when Hilda was young. King Edwin was killed in a battle on the Plain of Heathfield in 633. Bishop Paulinus fled with Queen Ethelburga and her daughter, but Hilda stayed behind. Oswald, who had been living in exile with the Irish monks of Iona, claimed the throne, and restored Christianity to Northumbria. Aidan, an Irish monk, became the bishop and Hilda's friend.

At the age of thirty-three, Hilda felt called to the cloister. She wanted to go to France, where her sister, a widow and the mother of King Aldwulf of East Anglia, was a professed nun. Bishop Aidan encouraged her to stay in England by giving her property for a monastery in Northumbria on the bank of the River Wear. Ten years later, she founded a monastery for monks and nuns at Whitby. The men and women lived in separate communities but they worshipped together. Often an abbess presided over a double monastery. This was an age when it was possible for a woman to be superior of both female and male monastics. Today we might even acknowledge her as having held the position of a seminary rector. Bede tells us, "Those under her direction were required to make a thorough study of the Scriptures and occupy themselves in good works, to such good effect that many were found fitted for Holy Orders and the service of God's altar." Bede names five of her monks who became bishops.

Her monastic community loved her and so did everyone else, Bede assures us: "Christ's servant Abbess Hilda, whom all her acquaintances called Mother because of her wonderful devotion and grace, brought about the amendment and salvation of many living far distant, who heard the inspiring story of her industry and goodness." Hilda was so prudent and wise that kings, as well as ordinary folk, consulted her. They all asked for her advice and took it, Bede reports.

The story I like best about Hilda is how she became the patroness of the first reputable poet of the English language. She was a refined lady who entertained with *soirees* at Whitby. Poets and musicians were invited by her to perform at the monastery, especially on feasts. Caedmon, a swineherd at Whitby, was no companion of this crowd. Whenever he saw the harp being brought out, he retreated to the barn to sit with the pigs rather than with the poets and musicians. One night an angel, disguised as a man, appeared to Caedmon in his sleep and asked him to sing some verses. Caedmon protested that he was unlearned in that art, but the angel coaxed verses from him in praise of God the Creator. In the morning, Caedmon could remember the poetry he had composed in the night. Hilda was informed of this marvel, and she was delighted. Whitby was a place of learning, a center of culture, and Abbess Hilda now had a poet-in-residence. Look up Caedmon in most English literature textbooks, and there you will find his "Hymn to Creation" on the first page.

Hilda and her community were so well respected that in 663 a synod was held at Whitby. She participated in it along with two kings, several bishops, and an abbot. They all met to discuss the Irish issue. The Irish were still celebrating Easter on a different Sunday than the Christians of Roman observance. The Irish persisted in having their own liturgical practices and monastic customs. The problem was that both expressions of Christianity prevailed in England. Pope Gregory probably wouldn't have considered this a controversy. He'd favored borrowing from whatever was good in various churches. "Let the mind of the English grow accustomed to it," was the advice he'd given to the missionaries he sent from Rome (Bede).

Now, however, Wilfrid, the English Abbot of Ripon, who had been educated by Irish monks, wanted unity of practices and argued for the Roman ways he had come to accept. Colman, the Irish Bishop of Lindisfarne, argued for the Irish ways. Wilfrid asked Colman how people from such an insignificant island like Ireland could place themselves above the laws of the universal church. The Romanists won out. Hilda must have been disappointed. She favored the Celtic form of Christianity, having been formed in the religion by an Irish bishop. After the Synod of Whitby, the English Church became more uniformly Roman, as did Hilda's monastery. And eventually the Irish conformed to the Church of Rome.

It is apparent that many nuns began following the Rule of St. Benedict in the seventh century. There are editions of the Rule from this period in which the nouns have been feminized. The double monastery was common by the sixth century, but very few were left by the ninth. Communities of Benedictine women remained in separate existence.

An abbess wore a ring and cross. She carried a crozier (staff) in ceremony, and had a mitre (hat), but didn't wear it on top of her veil. Some abbesses wore a stole to administer blessings. All of them sat on thrones in their abbey churches. They had ecclesiastical powers that are forbidden to women today. Medieval abbesses published mandates, dedicated churches, installed priests, presided over tribunals, and hosted councils, as Hilda did at Whitby.

Cuthbert

The Life of St. Cuthbert is one of the several biographies written by Bede. Cuthbert was born in Northumbria in 634, fifty years before his biographer. Unlike Bede, who probably never went far beyond the borders of his monastery's property, Cuthbert traveled all around England.

Cuthbert was an athletic youngster and boasted of winning all the games he played with his childhood chums. One day on their playing field, a child of three approached these older boys who were engaged in the sports of wrestling, running, and jumping over hedges. The little tyke picked out Cuthbert for a scolding. He upbraided him for this wild behavior that was so unbefitting of a priest and bishop. From that time on Cuthbert became less rowdy and more serious, because he understood the child's prophecy.

When he was old enough, Cuthbert entered the Abbey of Melrose, where it was observed that he worked and prayed harder than the other monks. St. Benedict would have been proud of him because at table in the refectory, Cuthbert did not drink wine. In his day—the sixth century—Benedict couldn't convince monks to abstain from it. Cuthbert did not hold back from food, however. He was in good shape physically, and he attributed this to the nutritious meals he ate.

Cuthbert attended the Council of Whitby, and argued for the use of Roman practice in the church instead of the Irish ways. He said the Irish only thought they knew what was right.

At the age of thirty, he became the prior of the monastery on the Isle of Lindisfarne. This was still a dependency of Melrose Abbey, and Cuthbert represented Abbot Eata in ruling over the community. The monks gave him a cool reception, but he won them over by his kindness and patience. "At chapter meetings he was often worn down by bitter insults, but would put an end to the arguments simply by rising and walking out, calm and unruffled. Next day he would give the same people exactly the same admonitions, as though there had been no unpleasantness the previous day" (Farmer). Bede says that when the monks confessed their sins to him, he was so overcome with sympathy for their weaknesses that instead of imposing the penance on the errant monks, he performed it himself.

In 681, Cuthbert was made Bishop of Lindisfarne. He was a wise and faithful shepherd, but the burden of his bishopric was too much for him. After five years, he resigned and went back to being a monk. Bede records several miracles attributed to St. Cuthbert, citing the sources. Bede was a careful historian, always crediting the people from whom he heard these accounts, and asking them to read his drafts. "I have tried to avoid all ambiguity or hair-splitting and to write a clear investigation of the truth in simple terms," Bede stated to the Bishop of Lindisfarne, who had commissioned the biography of Cuthbert.

The Abbot of Lindisfarne at the time Bede was researching Cuthbert's life reported a miracle that brought immense relief to a monk named Wahlstod. This monk was assisting the ill and dying Cuthbert back to his cell one day. As soon as Wahlstod touched the holy man, he felt himself healed of an old complaint—diarrhea. Bede records this verbatim as he heard it from Abbot Herefrith.

Cuthbert wanted to be buried in a remote place on the island. He told the monks it would be to their advantage if he were not buried at the monastery because they would never have any rest from the pilgrims who would come to pray at his tomb. The monks pleaded with him for the privilege of having his remains in the monastery. He gave in to them, providing they placed him in a not too prominent spot. Cuthbert's remains did not stay on Lindisfarne. They were transferred to the mainland. His bones rest in Durham where his biographer's remains were brought from Jarrow Abbey in 1050. Durham, once a Benedictine monastery, is now an Anglican cathedral. Pilgrims of both the Church of England and Church of Rome, as well as many other people, go there to pay honor to Cuthbert and Bede.

Our community once had a Cuthbert and a Bede. It's been customary in these latter years not to change our names upon entering the monastery. I don't suppose we'll ever have another Cuthbert or another Bede. I regret the passing of these great Benedictine names from among us.

Father Cuthbert was my confessor sometimes. He was a gentle, happy man. Although silence was supposed to be observed in the corridors of the monastery, I remember him walking by my room whistling and snapping his fingers. His usual greeting when meeting you face to face was "Pax!" After I'd made my confessions to him and he'd said the words of absolution, Father Cuthbert would tell me, "Go in peace and sin no more. Ha!"

Finding himself in a generation gap after Vatican Council II, he disliked some of the changes that grabbed the attention of the young monks in the 1960s and 1970s. "If the haunting echo of the organ leaves them unmoved while the plunk of a guitar can set them off in ecstasy, let's not get excited," he said. When informed of the price we had paid for the pipe organ in our new church, he replied, "Wow! For that amount we could have bought two thousand guitars."

Willibrord, Willibald, Wunibald, Walburga, and Winfrid

*C*an you repeat their names lickety-split? Although one might think these are members of a contemporary law firm, this is not the case. They are all Anglo-Saxon monastics who became missionaries on the Continent. Wunibald and Willibald were brothers and their sister was Walburga. They were related to Willibrord and Winfrid, whose name was changed to Boniface.

Alcuin of York wrote the life of Willibrord, who baptized Charlemagne's father, Pepin the Short. An English monk, Alcuin met Charlemagne in 781, and was asked by him to establish a school at Aachen. The Holy Roman Emperor himself was one of the students.

Willibrord was born in Northumbria in 658. The night of his conception, his mother dreamed that she had swallowed the moon. The parish priest told her that the moon was a symbol of her son. "By the brightness of his fame and the beauty of his life, he will attract to himself the eyes of the multitudes." If the boy was told this, he must have wondered how it would all come about when, at the age of reason, he was taken to the monastery at Ripon. In adulthood, he began to ponder his situation: was it more important to seek self-sanctification in the monastery or to be a missionary? "He had heard that in the northern regions of the world the harvest was great but the laborers few" (Talbot). Thus it was that his mother's dream was fulfilled when he set sail for Friesland in 690.

He was made Bishop of Utrecht, and is recognized now as the Apostle of the Low Countries. On a visitation of the monastery he founded at Echternach in Luxemburg, Willibrord went around to all the monks' cells and the other rooms in order to see what improvements could be made. In the storeroom he found only a small supply of wine. Willibrord blessed the cask, and that night wine rose to the top and overflowed onto the floor. In the morning, the monastery steward informed the bishop of the miracle. Willibrord told him not to tell this to anyone else until after his death. His reputation as a distributor of wine would have no doubt put him in popular demand at many monasteries.

Hunebric, a nun, wrote the biography of Willibald. She prefaced her work with an apology: "I know that it may seem very bold on my part to write this book when there are so many holy priests capable of doing better." This is not the kind of statement Hilda of Whitby would have made. The biography begins with Hunebric's describing the baby in his cradle as "a loveable little creature" (Talbot). Willibald almost died at the age of three. His parents promised to offer him to a monastery if he survived the disease. They took him to one when he was five, but he did not remain in monastic life.

As a young man, he longed to go on a pilgrimage to Rome and the Holy Land. Convincing his father and brother Wunibald to accompany him, they set sail from England. The father died in Lucca, and both brothers contracted the plague in Rome. After they had recovered, Wunibald decided to stay in Rome and become a monk. Willibald traveled for another ten years. He is believed to have been the first Englishman to tour the Holy Land. Upon his return to Italy, Willibald entered St. Benedict's monastery at Monte Cassino, where he remained ten years.

A guest of the abbey asked Willibald to go with him to Rome. At an audience with the Pope, it was suggested to Willibald that he might like to join his fellow countryman and relative, Bishop Boniface, in Germany. Willibald consented and was consecrated Bishop of Eichstätt. His brother was in Germany by now and so was their sister, Walburga. Bishop Willibald founded a double monastery at Heidenheim, installing Wunibald as its first abbot. Walburga succeeded him in office. Hunebric, a Heidenheim nun, wrote about all of them.

Tetta and Leoba

*L*eoba was already a nun at the double Abbey of Wimborne when her relative Walburga arrived. Both of them were destined for missionary work in Germany.

Rudolph of Fulda wrote the life of Leoba, and in it he tells a story about Wimborne when Tetta was abbess. A certain nun was more strict and disciplined than the others, and Tetta often appointed her to positions of authority in the monastery. The younger sisters disliked her because she was such an old shrew. When the nun died and was buried, the young ones stomped on her grave, cursing her dead body. The mound of dirt over the grave sunk six inches from all their trampling.

Abbess Tetta was alarmed when she heard of this behavior. She chastised the young nuns for being so hard-hearted and unforgiving. As a penance, they were to fast for three days and say special prayers for the repose of the nun's soul. At the end of the third day, the dirt rose to a level surface.

Boniface, Leoba's kinsman, personally asked her to come to Germany. Tetta reluctantly let her go. Boniface appointed Leoba to head the abbey at Bischofsheim. She had the characteristics Benedict lists for a superior. Rudolf says, "She was ever on her guard not to teach others what she did not carry out herself. In her conduct there was no arrogance or pride; she was no distinguisher of persons, but showed herself affable and kindly to all" (Talbot).

She was so well loved that none of her young nuns complained when they had to read to her from the Bible at nap time. When it appeared that the abbess had dozed off, the nuns would test her by skipping a word or mispronouncing one. Leoba always detected their trick.

Rudolf relates an incident that brought scandal to the nuns of Bischofsheim. A crippled girl who begged alms from the monastery became pregnant. When the baby was born, she drowned the child in a stream on the monastery property—a stream used by the townspeople. A woman discovered the infant's body, and she began spreading the rumor that one of the nuns had functioned as both mother and priest by giving birth to the baby and then baptizing it in the river. Look for the one who is missing, she told the citizens, and you'll find the nun who is responsible for this crime. The whole town was in an uproar.

Leoba called the nuns together and told them of the predicament they were facing because Sister Agatha had gone to visit her parents. A message was sent advising her to return immediately because of the charge being made against her. Referring to Sacred Scripture, Agatha prayed that like Susanna she would be spared from this false accusation. The abbess had the nuns recite the whole Psalter three times a day. Finally, the guilty party confessed.

Leoba had a reputation for hospitality. She welcomed all visitors as Christ himself by washing their feet. Even when she was fasting, orders were given to prepare a banquet for guests. Cousin Boniface was always a very special guest of hers, and she received the same attention whenever she visited him at the monastery in Fulda. By his decree, she was allowed into the cloister of his all male monastery. They spent the day visiting, and she departed for Bischofsheim in early evening. Shortly before his death, Boniface visited Leoba and asked her to never leave Germany. She is buried in the church at Fulda, and Rudolph ends his biography by commenting: "These two, though they do not share a tomb, yet lie in one place and never fail to look on those who seek their intercession" (Talbot).

Boniface

Willibald was privileged to write the biography of the great Boniface, whose presence in Germany accounted for all of these monks and nuns, some of them his relatives, leaving their English homeland to assist him in the conversion of the Germans. We had a German monk, Brother Felix, in this monastery who had no appreciation for the English, and he didn't like being reminded that the patron saint of Germany came from England.

Boniface's biographer records the incredible fact that at the age of four or five, the boy Winfrid—as he was known then—had "subdued the flesh to the spirit and meditated on the things that are eternal rather than on those that are temporal" (Talbot). Priests who visited the family were astounded by his ability to speak with them about theological matters.

Young Winfrid asked to enter a monastery, but his father did not approve. He promised the boy an early inheritance if he stayed home. This was of no interest to Winfrid. He went to Exeter and spent the remaining years of his youth there. He was a zealous student with a special love for studying Scripture. Willibald says this was "a marvelous protection against the enticements and diabolical suggestions which beset young men in the flower of their youth." Are we to presume the boy never had an impure thought?

When he reached adulthood, Winfrid taught Scripture in the monastery school of Nursling. "As a teacher, he was a model, because he did not refuse to learn from his pupils." Besides teaching, he performed daily manual labor and fulfilled all the other monastic obligations. "He applied himself assiduously, as the Rule of Benedict prescribes."

Although he was living a happy life in this English monastery, after his ordination at the age of thirty the call to the missions appealed to him. He left for Friesland in 718. Bishop Willibrord thought Winfrid would be his ideal successor in Utrecht, and told him this could be arranged, but Winfrid protested. When Pope Gregory II summoned him to Rome, Winfrid went without objecting, and could not turn down the assignment the pontiff had for him. Renamed for a Roman martyr on whose feast day Gregory made him a bishop, Boniface became the Apostle of Germany.

Boniface won converts initially by chopping down the sacred oak tree of the Hessians, and he used the lumber to build a church dedicated to St. Peter the Apostle. Like Augustine of Canterbury, who had been sent to England by an earlier Pope Gregory, Boniface also depended on Rome for answers to his problems. In one letter, Boniface asked if he should dine with certain misbehaving priests and bishops. Pope Gregory II replied, "Do not refuse to eat and speak with them at the same table. It often happens that where correction fails to bring men to an acknowledgement of the truth, the constant and gentle persuasion of their table companions leads them back to the paths of goodness."

In later years, Boniface was assigned to reforming the church of the Franks. He found their priesthood in sad decline. What made matters even worse, he reported, was that some of these debased priests had become bishops. As bishops they denied the charges of fornication and adultery, but remained "shiftless drunkards, addicted to the chase." They actually engaged in armed combat, ending up with the blood of both Christians and unbelievers on their hands. It wasn't all that easy fostering social companionship with these clerical reprobates.

In a letter to the Archbishop of Canterbury, Boniface informed him of some of the changes he made among the Frankish clergy. "We have forbidden the clergy to hunt, to go about in the woods with dogs and to keep falcons or hawks." He shaped up the clergy and hierarchy of the Franks, and then he had some words to say about the English. Boniface asked the Archbishop of Canterbury to prohibit English matrons and nuns from traveling back and forth to Rome. A good number of them were falling by the wayside. "There are many towns in Lombardy and Gaul where there is not a courtesan or a harlot but is of English stock" (Talbot). Finally in 791 a church council forbade nuns from making pilgrimages, but the damage to the reputation of nuns was done.

One of the most famous nuns from the past is not a real person but a figment of Geoffrey Chaucer's imagination who went on pilgrimage to Canterbury in the Middle Ages and told two tales along the way, one the story of St. Cecilia and the other the story of a debauched priest. Among Chaucer's pilgrims to Canterbury there was also a monk who scorned the Rule of Benedict for being old-fashioned. He loved hunting and saw no need for doing manual labor or reading in his cell. He said the old adage that a monk out of his cloister was like a fish out of water was worthless. No one was trying to keep him in his cloister. In 1298 Pope Boniface VIII laid down the law that nuns were to remain in their cloisters perpetually. These strict reforms never had much success, as perhaps the tales, written a century after Pope Boniface's decree, demonstrate.

Boniface functioned as a bishop for thirty-six years, having built many monasteries and churches, and established bishoprics at Cologne and Mainz. He was martyred while on a confirmation trip in 754. He never returned to his homeland, but he kept up a correspondence with English prelates, monks, nuns, and royalty. One of the monarchs, King Ethelbert of Kent, asked Boniface to send him some falcons from Germany. Perhaps he sent falcons that had been confiscated from priests.

The Hospitable Meinrad

Meinrad was a hermit who lived at a place in Switzerland called Einsiedeln. Formerly, he had taught literature and Scripture at the monastic school of Reichenau. When he went off to become a hermit, he took with him a missal, a breviary, the Rule of St. Benedict, and the writings of John Cassian, the fourth-century monk whose work Benedict admired.

Early in the year 861, two guests called at Meinrad's hermitage. Although hermits strive to live alone with God, they are seldom left alone. Someone is always coming to them for spiritual direction or hospitality. So, Meinrad welcomed his visitors even though he'd had a premonition that these two men had come to harm him. They intended to rob Meinrad of the riches that they imagined he had received from genuine pilgrims. Meinrad prepared a meal for his visitors, after which they bludgeoned him to death with clubs. He died as the result of his hospitality.

Meinrad's two pet ravens attacked the thieving murderers and drove them from the hermitage, pursuing them all the way to Zurich where they were arrested for the crime. Eventually, the Abbey of Einsiedeln was built on the site of Meinrad's martyrdom. In the thirteenth century, admission was restricted to the sons of nobility. At the beginning of the fifteenth century, there were only three monks left in the community. By the time of the Reformation, there was only one monk, and he took leave to follow Ulrich Zwingli. The abbey recovered when it was no longer under royal patronage, and is today the largest house in the Swiss Congregation of Benedictines.

Benedict has a whole chapter in his Rule devoted to hospitality. He says every guest should be welcomed as Christ. This is an obligation we can't ignore. Sometimes monks are guests of other monasteries. St. Benedict tells them how to behave, cautioning them not to make "excessive demands that upset the monastery" (*RB* 61.2). When Brother Sebastian and I were novices, we were assigned to look after an elderly monk of another monastery who visited here occasionally. He wanted to take some of his meals in his room, and my classmate and I carried them to him. His demands were never excessive, but the amount of snuff he spilled all over the room and in the bed, where he partook of breakfast, was abundant. The only criticism I ever knew him to make was with regard to a book in our library. He suggested that we remove *Kristin Lavransdatter* because he considered it immoral. We did not take his suggestion about this classic novel by Sigrid Undset set in medieval Norway. On one of his visits, he took ill and had to be hospitalized. He died far from his own monastery.

Hubert Van Zeller, in his commentary on the Rule, says, "The surest way for a visiting monk to alienate the sympathies of his hosts is to tell them how much more convenient they will find it if they sing or cook or save money or ventilate and heat the place as he suggests."

Benedict rolls out the carpet for the visiting monk. If the visitor is satisfied, "he should be received for as long a time as he wishes" (*RB* 61.3).I myself have been a guest at monasteries in this country and abroad. Arriving at Maria Laach, I asked the porter, "Sprechen Sie Englisch?" He answered in my native tongue, "No. This is Germany. We speak German in this country." When the guest master arrived, he said he could speak a little English: "Open the door, shut the window, what time does the train leave?" He told me lunch was served at noon. "Wait here. I'll come back to take you to the refectory. We cannot be late." I went for a short walk, and got lost in the woods. Of course I arrived late for the meal. When I was ushered in, all the Maria Laach monks took notice of me, and so did members of Germany's parliament who were at the abbey on retreat.

French Unity and Purity:
Another St. Benedict and the Cluniacs

Benedict of Aniane was a very ascetical monk, but one who fled the monastery when it became evident that the monks wanted him for abbot. He went home to Aniane and built a hermitage for himself.

Charlemagne remained faithful to the Benedictines, to the point of granting them the privilege of being the only kind of monastics in his realm. Obtaining a copy of the Holy Rule from Monte Cassino, he had it copied and distributed so that there would be uniformity in all the monasteries. He also instructed every community to use the same kind of scale for weighing the daily pound of bread St. Benedict had prescribed, and a container that would measure out a *hemina* of wine, the amount St. Benedict allowed each monk daily. Some scholars believe a *hemina* is a quart, which doesn't seem unreasonable for Italians.

The Emperor did not complete his task of unification, but his son, Louis the Pious, took over. In 817 at Aachen, Louis gave Benedict of Aniane authority over all of the monasteries in the Empire and installed him as the Abbot of Inde. In this case, he was chosen by the Emperor and not elected by monks. Benedict established eighty norms and customs to be held in common by all Benedictines. He had monks abandon agriculture. Serfs took over the farming while the monks concentrated on arts and crafts inside the monastery. Additional liturgical prayers and ceremonies were introduced.

Monasticism as shaped by Benedict of Aniane went into decline, however. When the monasteries grew wealthy, lax adherence to the Rule often followed, and many were disillusioned. By the year 909 there was another monastic movement on the scene—the Cluniacs—that resulted in a resurgence in monastic life in France. William of Aquitane gave twelve monks from the abbeys of Baume and Gigny an estate in Burgundy on which to build a monastery. He wanted them to pray for him in reparation for a murder he had committed. He'd been reluctant to give them this particular piece of property because it had a good hunting ground. But Berno, the abbot, told him to replace his hunting dogs with monks. Praying monks would be more beneficial to him and of greater service to God than barking dogs.

This French abbey was the dominant influence in continental monasticism for several centuries. Its stricter adherence to the Rule of Benedict was immediately embraced in this era of reform. There were many abbots of Cluny, but five are remembered as great saints: Odo, Maiol, Odilo, Hugh, and Peter the Venerable.

Odo, the second abbot, had a sense of humor and kept his monks in laughter. He could also move them to tears. Maiol joined Cluny in order to evade being made Bishop of Besancon. As Abbot of Cluny, he was offered the papacy by Emperor Otto II, but Maiol declined. Odilo succeeded Maiol and reigned fifty-five years. He reformed many monasteries and brought them under Cluny's control. Hugh, the builder of the great abbey church (the largest in Christendom until the construction of St. Peter's in Rome), expanded Cluny's influence by founding monasteries in Italy, Spain, and England. At the time of Hugh's death in 1109, the number of Cluniac monasteries totaled 1,184. There were also communities of nuns affiliated with Cluny. Abbot Hugh's sister, Ermengarde, was the abbess in the first nuns' monastery. His mother joined the community, and so did the mother of Peter the Venerable.

Peter the Venerable, the last of the saintly abbots of Cluny, battled with Bernard of Clairvaux and other Cistercians, members of a stricter reform movement who disagreed with him over issues of monastic observance. He also had to contend with Abbot Pons, his predecessor in the abbey. The Cistercians were critical of the Benedictines for wearing garments made of silk and linen under their habits and for lining their habits with fur. They dined on a variety of courses in their refectories, and they not only ate meat but also used lard rendered from the fat of four-footed animals. All of this was contrary to the purity of St. Benedict's Rule.

Although Bernard was forceful in his charges of monastic impropriety in Cluniac monasteries, he could also be mellow. He told his Cistercian monks who were complaining about the Cluniac custom of eating meat, contrary to the Rule of Benedict, that they should remember Adam and Eve were expelled from Paradise not for eating meat but fruit. Bernard's verbal and epistolary exchanges with Peter the Venerable were gentlemanly.

Abbot Pons was not a gentleman. His intention was to take back Cluny by force. Hearing that Abbot Peter was conducting visitations of monasteries in Aquitaine, Pons gathered together a band of roughnecks to storm the abbey. He kicked out all the monks loyal to Peter, and tortured others into submitting to him. Pons brought women into the cloister, and enlisted local knights to protect the monastery along with the villages and granges that he confiscated from Cluny. In order to pay his protectors, Pons melted down all the precious chalices, reliquaries, and candlesticks.

After several months, the pope intervened. Ordered to appear in Rome, Pons refused to leave Cluny. He and his followers were excommunicated, but that made no impression on Pons. He rebutted the pontiff by telling him only St. Peter in heaven was authorized to excommunicate. Pons eventually went to Rome with Peter the Venerable. The affair was settled by putting Pons in the Papal Prison where he died of a fever.

There were not many praises sung for Pons, but the monks of Cluny may have appreciated his accomplishments in collecting relics. When he was the legitimate Abbot of Cluny, he procured a finger of Stephen, the first martyr, and a tooth of John the Baptist.

The Cluniac novice was instructed how to bow and genuflect, when to sit and when to stand, how to chant and how to intone, when to allow the hands outside the sleeves of the habit and when to put them back in, how to dress and undress, and how to indicate by sign language what food or drink he wanted passed to him at meals. These were mostly the same things taught to our novitiate class in the middle of the twentieth century.

Today, near the ruins of Cluny, there stands another monastery. It is called Taizé.

Bernard and Cistercian Reform

On Palm Sunday in 1098, twenty-one monks left their French Cluniac monastery in order to keep their vows according to the Rule of Benedict as he intended it to be lived. Their new monastery was established at Citeaux, and they became known as Cistercians. These monks rejected whatever they found contrary to St. Benedict's teachings and desired to live by his rule literally. They felt the monks back at Molesmes and in all the other Benedictine monasteries had become too lax, too soft. Cistercian Bernard of Claivaux was right to criticize the Cluniacs for their luxuries and laxity. Just as Cluniacs were a reform of the Benedictines, the Cistercians were one of many further reforms.

The nature of the Cistercian reform was a return to simplicity. The Divine Office was restored to the manner prescribed by the Rule, and churches were stripped of excessive adornment. The monks dressed themselves less elegantly than the Benedictines, shunning fur-lined garb, but wearing warm habits woven from the wool of their sheep. The Cistercians avoided making commitments to secular rulers, and they supported themselves by manual labor. These monks developed the lay brother system so successfully that the Cistercians, too, eventually became wealthy. The brothers earned an income for the monasteries by farming the vast granges they owned.

Although they wanted to recapture both the spirit and the letter of Benedict's Rule, the Cistercians departed from one of the patriarch's provisions: they did not accept boy oblates. Bernard of Clairvaux had a young relative named Robert who went to Cluny, and then to Citeaux, and then back to Cluny. Such a maverick upset Bernard. He insisted that Robert be returned to the monks of Citeaux. The Benedictines insisted that Robert had been given to them by his parents. Bernard objected. The ritual according to the Rule of Benedict had been performed illegally. The boy's hands had not been wrapped in the altar cloth. Besides, Bernard asked, what is common sense: a boy unwillingly offered to a monastery by his parents or a young man who enters of his own volition? Furthermore, if Robert had truly been offered to the Benedictines, what was he doing outside the monastery? Bernard reminded him it was the world—not Cluny—from which he came to Citeaux.

The three founders of the Cistercians are Saints Robert of Molesmes, Alberic, and Stephen Harding. The monks of Molesmes found that they could not live without Robert. And after he was only a year away from them, they petitioned the pope to send him back. Robert returned to the Benedictine monastery and ruled it for another twelve years. Alberic succeeded him as Abbot of Citeaux. Stephen Harding, an Englishman, saw the publication of the Charter of Charity, the guidelines for the order. During his time in office an illness took the lives of many monks. The community was practically decimated. Help was on the way, however. Bernard entered the monastery in 1112, along with thirty of his friends and relatives. Citeaux was able to make ten foundations by 1119. One of them was at Clairvaux, where twenty-four-year-old Bernard became its first abbot.

Stephen Harding was reluctant to admit women into the order, but it was inevitable that Benedictine women would also want to reform themselves. In 1132, nuns from Jully founded the first monastery of Cistercian women. By the middle of the thirteenth century, there were nine hundred nunneries. Each community had an abbess, but an abbot was appointed to conduct visitations, preside at elections, and make sure the nuns were provided for materially. They were cloistered, but operated schools for girls. In the beginning, lay brothers were provided to do manual labor, but this became a burden for the men who already had enough work to do in their own monasteries. Lay sisters were instituted in 1222.

Throughout history, Benedictines themselves have had to renew their order after periods of great decline. It has been our saints who have helped us out of these slumps. Also, renewal is an ongoing process for those who follow the Rule of St. Benedict. Benedict calls this conversion (*conversatio*), and it never ends as long as we struggle on this earth. The Rule calls attention to our laxity and reminds us how to achieve fidelity.

When I was in Ireland, I visited Holy Cross Abbey, which was a Benedictine monastery before the Cistercian monks took possession of it in 1180. In penal times, Queen Elizabeth gave the monastic buildings and lands to her cousin, the Earl of Ormond. A monk was retained, however, as the caretaker. Catholic pilgrims, much to the annoyance of the English, continued venerating the relic of Christ's cross kept at the abbey. Eventually, the place was abandoned, and it fell into a state of collapse. In the eighteenth century, local people began using the site as a cemetery. In 1971 a restoration began, and Holy Cross Abbey became a pilgrimage center once more. This time, instead of monks, diocesan priests are in charge.

Holy Cross Abbey has been restored to its medieval Cistercian simplicity. St. Bernard of Clairvaux had complained about the kinds of churches the Benedictines built. "O vanity of vanities," he said with regard to Benedictine architecture. "No, insanity rather than vanity" (Knowles). I waited in the cloister walk before entering the church, which was being used for a wedding with a bishop presiding. After the matrimonial party had departed, the church was all mine. I marveled at the Gothic arches and the clean lime-washed walls. I climbed the night stairs that the medieval monks had used coming from their dormitory to chant Matins at two in the morning. The medieval storeroom (cellars) is now a gift shop, and the lay brothers' dormitory has become a tearoom. I lingered there with a cup of tea and a scone, gazing out the window at the green, green courtyard below.

Back on the bus that had brought me to Holy Cross Abbey, the driver asked, "How did you like the abbey, Brother?"

"It's wonderful," I replied. "But I think it should be given back to monks."

"You didn't take good care of it when you had it," he retorted.

I recalled having read a book concerning visitations of Irish Cistercian monasteries in the early part of the thirteenth century. The visitator had observed shabby conditions in the monastic houses, and at Holy Cross Abbey the crucifix over the high altar was in need of repair.

By the end of the twelfth century, Cistercians had become wealthy through their own efforts and because they had begun accepting benefices. There was a loss of contemplative spirit. A reform of the Cistercians would occur in the seventeenth century at a site in France called La Trappe. In 1664, Abbot Armand-Jean de Rance found the monastery of La Trappe terribly dilapidated and dirty. A bailiff and his family lived in one wing of the monastery. The seven monks slept wherever there was no leak in the roof, stairways had collapsed, and the walls were cracked. The refectory was being used as a bowling alley, but things were about to change. Monks of the Order of Cistercians of Strict Observance came to be known as Trappists.

Shortly before I left Ireland, I was pleased to discover a ruined Cistercian abbey near a town where I was staying for a few days. A barbed wire fence surrounded it, and cows were pasturing within the confines of Hore Abbey. The gate was padlocked. I was determined to reach the abbey because I wanted to pray Lauds in the place where medieval monks had chanted their psalms. It was the feast of St. Gregory the Great, the monk who had become a pope and after whom Gregorian chant is named.

I climbed the fence. Avoiding the cow pies, I crossed the wet pasture. Again I had come upon Cistercian simplicity. There was enough of a limestone chapel left to shelter me from the September wind, and I eagerly anticipated settling down with my breviary. From the ruins, a middle-aged couple emerged. The man, carrying a camera, said, "*Guten morgen!*"

Friends of the Order

St. Henry was related to Charlemagne, and became the Holy Roman Emperor himself in 1014. In his youth, Henry was attracted to monastic life, but the abbot of Saint-Vanne convinced him that his vocation was not to the cloister but to the world. He was destined by God to be a secular ruler.

Henry had a wife who is often ignored when we recall the saintly members of our Benedictine family. Poor Cunnegunda! The mere pronunciation of her name (Cooney-goon-da) causes laughter nowadays. She was a noble Luxemburger who married Henry when he was the Duke of Bavaria. Cunnegunda was accused of being unfaithful to her husband, and Henry believed her detractors. To prove her innocence, Cunnegunda walked over red-hot ploughshares in her bare feet. Henry was ashamed of himself for having had misgivings about his wife. Her feet weren't even blistered by the red-hot ploughshares.

This royal couple looked kindly upon the Benedictines and assisted them by founding new monasteries for men and for women, and by reforming other monastic houses that had fallen into negligence. The monks and nuns of the monasteries established by Henry and Cunnegunda had their own troubles. Some did not want to accept the reforms Henry thought suitable for monastic renewal. Then there was the problem at Kaufungen. This was a community of nuns founded by Cunnegunda in response to a vow she'd made upon her recovery from a serious illness. Cunnegunda was extremely fond of her niece Judith, having overseen her education with the intention of making her an abbess one day. Judith got Kaufungen Abbey along with good advice from her aunt on how to run a nunnery.

Soon reports reached Cunnegunda regarding the behavior of Abbess Judith. The abbess was always the first into the refectory, and the last to arrive at chapel. She was frivolous and lax. She delighted in hearing gossip and spreading it. Cunnegunda spoke to her niece about these things, but the young abbess was obviously not impressed. Cunnegunda could tolerate no more nonsense. One day Judith was absent from a Sunday procession, and when Cunnegunda found her banqueting with some of the young nuns, she slapped Abbess Judith's face so hard that the marks of Cunnegunda's fingers were imprinted on Judith's face until her dying day.

In 1021, Henry was returning from a military campaign when he became ill while visiting Monte Cassino. It was presumed that St. Benedict's intercession restored him to health, although Henry was left with a lame foot for the rest of his life. After his death, Cunnegunda became a nun at Kaufungen, taking the lowest place in the community. She spent the last fifteen years of her life in the cloister. On her deathbed, she was aware that the nuns were preparing a funeral pall trimmed in gold for her. She could not die in peace until they promised not to use it.

St. Frances of Rome was another laywoman who was attracted to our Order. She was born in 1384 in that part of the Eternal City known as Trastevere. Frances was the daughter of wealthy nobles. At the age of twelve, Frances was betrothed to Lorenzo Ponziano and she became his teenage bride the following year. Lorenzo's brother had a wife named Vannozza. She and Frances became good friends. They had both wanted to become brides of the church, but here they were with earthly husbands.

Frances and Vannozza were concerned about the poor and sick Romans, and began ministering to them in their hovels and at hospitals. Their mother-in-law was disturbed by this charitable work. She worried that it would interfere with the obligations of their social lives. The husbands, however, had no objections. When Mother Ponziano died, Frances's father-in-law asked her to assume charge of the household. She declined, observing that the duty should go to Vannozza who was married to the older Ponziano brother. Vannozza refused the offer, too, and it went back to Frances, who accepted the burden this time. She treated the servants of this rich extended family with respect, as if they were siblings, her biographer reports. Although this was a wealthy family with servants, Frances still had demands from the household and her husband to which she had to respond. Frances believed that a wife should be devoted to God, but that sometimes she had to leave off her prayer and go to find God in the ordinary duties of a housewife.

Frances was the mother of two sons, John Baptist and Evangelist, and a daughter, Agnes. Evangelist and Agnes died young during a plague, but John Baptist grew to manhood, and married Mobilia, who had a violent temper, and was overbearing in other ways. She despised Frances, ridiculed her mother-in-law in public, and complained about her to John Baptist and his father. Still, when Mobilia became seriously ill, it was Frances who patiently nursed her daughter-in-law back to health.

The Ponziano family became embroiled in papal politics. Supporting the legitimate pope resulted in the loss of family property; the crops at their farm in Campagna were burned and the flocks destroyed. Frances's husband was wounded in battle, her brother-in-law arrested, and her son taken hostage. The house in Rome was plundered. Of course, all these bad things could just as well have happened to them if they had been supporting the illegitimate pope, given the nature of papal politics in those days.

After all the turmoil came to an end, Lorenzo Ponziano was a broken man, physically and psychologically. Frances cared for her husband until his death, and then she went to live with the society of women she had founded. These women, dedicated to serving the poor and sick, followed the Rule of St. Benedict without professing monastic vows. One of them described how Frances treated the poor. "She used to go to the Campo Santo with food and rich delicacies to be distributed to the needy. On her return home, she would bring pieces of worn-out clothes and unclean rags which she would wash lovingly and mend carefully, as if they were to be used for God himself. The she would fold them carefully and perfume them."

In 1440, Frances took sick and went to live in the home of her son, dying there seven days after her arrival. She was buried in the Church of Santa Maria Nuova, which is in the care of Benedictine monks to this day.

From the early days of our Order's existence lay people have associated themselves with particular Benedictine communities, and have applied the teachings of Benedict to their own lives. We call these people Oblates of St. Benedict.

If historians want to know why the Germans had no intention of harming the Abbey of Monte Cassino during World War II, it is because the German commander at that devastating battle was an Oblate of St. Benedict, affiliated with the Archabbey of Beuron in his homeland. General Frido Von Senger transported the moveable artwork from the abbey to Rome for safekeeping. Most of the monks were also evacuated. Nevertheless, he held onto the hope that the abbey would be spared. When the Allies bombed the Cradle of Western Monasticism beyond recognition, he shouted, "The idiots! They've done it after all."

Ethelwold, Oswald, and Dunstan

In England, three Benedictine monks all became bishops in the tenth century: Ethelwold, Oswald, and Dunstan. St. Ethelwold, a monk under Abbot Dunstan of Glastonbury, became Bishop of Winchester in 963. He was greatly disappointed when introduced to the priests of his cathedral. Some of them refused to offer Mass. Too many of the priests were gluttons and drunkards. Priestly celibacy was not yet mandated, but some clerics had married illegally, and then abandoned their wives for other women. Ethelwold replaced these cathedral canons with monks.

Oswald was ordained a secular priest, but became a monk soon afterwards at the Abbey of Fleury in France. He founded monasteries in England, and when he was named Bishop of Worcester, monks were welcomed to sing the offices in his cathedral. Unlike Ethelwold, though, Oswald retained some of the secular clergy.

Dunstan went to Glastonbury Abbey when he was a boy. Like Bede, he developed many talents. Dunstan was a writer, an illuminator of manuscripts, a musician, and a metalworker. He is the patron saint of jewelers. Teenagers might also benefit from his protection and intercession. Young Dunstan worried over skin problems.

While not under monastic vows but studying for holy orders, Dunstan was called to serve in the court of King Athelstan.

He did not get on well at court, and was accused of being lazy, of spending too much time reading pagan poets and writers. Expelled from court, and despairing of clerical life, he thought about marriage, but in 934 he became a monk at Glastonbury. Later he was ordained by his uncle, St. Alphege, Bishop of Winchester.

Ten years later, Dunstan became the Abbot of Glastonbury. Once again he earned the disfavor of royalty. Critical of King Edwy's lifestyle, Dunstan was exiled to Flanders. Edgar, when he ascended the throne, brought Dunstan home, and made him Bishop of Worcester and London, and then Archbishop of Canterbury in 959.

Dunstan and the two other Benedictine bishops, Ethelwold and Oswald, are associated with drawing up the *Regularius Concordia*. This was a customary that was followed by all the Benedictine houses of England. While adhering to the instructions of St. Benedict's Rule, it multiplied prayers and ceremonies that the Holy Patriarch would have probably thought unnecessary. From two o'clock in the morning until seven o'clock, the monks and nuns were in choir. Five hours of incessant prayer would drive people out of monasteries nowadays.

Of the charming legends about Dunstan, one predicted his future before his birth. His mother was in church on Candlemas Day when a breeze extinguished all the lighted candles in the hands of the congregation. Hers remained lit and the people were able to relight theirs from it. The child she was carrying would one day give light to all of England. Remember how Willibrord's pregnant mother dreamed of swallowing the moon?

Once when Dunstan, the silversmith, was making a chalice, the devil appeared to him disguised as a woman. He was annoyed at having his work interrupted, and caught the devil by the nose with a pair of red-hot tongs. Dunstan held on until the devil disappeared screaming. Another craft in which Dunstan excelled was embroidery. He made vestments, and one of his designs was so elegant that the Lady Ethelfreda asked to use it as a gown. Dunstan gave her permission, knowing she was a genuine woman and not the devil in disguise.

He composed hymns and built a pipe organ. His harp could play by itself, having been trained by the master. Or was it an angel who plucked the strings of Dunstan's harp?

Besides being the patron saint of craftsmen, Dunstan, for a long time in Devonshire, was venerated as the patron of brew masters. Many a glass was lifted to this saint who was reported to have had an immense taste for beer.

Dunstan was an outspoken critic of kings, clerics, and monks. He succeeded in reforming all of them, even if his efforts were not initially appreciated. Although he was charged with enforcing clerical celibacy, this Archbishop of Canterbury believed there were more pressing issues at hand. For a number of years the Church in England had been in a state of decline. King Alfred the Great lamented the fact that it was difficult to find a priest in his realm who knew Latin. Bishop Asser of Sherborne was saddened by the sorry condition of monasticism. He had thought perhaps no one was joining monasteries as a result of Viking invasions, but on second thought he attributed it to the laxity in monasteries and the affluence in society.

The times were ripe for a Dunstan of Canterbury. We don't celebrate the Feast of St. Dunstan in this monastery. Once, however, when the Episcopal clergy of the Diocese of South Dakota were here on retreat, I walked past the door to our church, and I heard their bishop praising St. Dunstan of Canterbury, whose feast it was.

Anselm of Canterbury

Although St. Anselm was not English, he became the Archbishop of Canterbury in 1093. Anselm was born at Aosta in Lombardy in 1033. His parents were like those of Assisi's most famous son: the father was preoccupied with the affairs of business and the mother with raising her boy to love God. At the age of fourteen, Anselm tried entering a monastery, but he was turned away because he didn't have his father's permission. When the mother died, friction developed between Anselm and his father. The young man left Italy and went to France where he studied in various schools. In 1059, he was drawn to the Abbey of Bec by the fame of Lanfranc, a monk and teacher who was also from Lombardy. Anselm entered the monastic community. In 1063 he was appointed prior, much to the displeasure of some senior monks who thought he was too young in monastic life for this office.

One of these elders carried his resentment into the infirmary. On his deathbed, he called for the presence of a monk to prepare him for the beyond. It was siesta time, but Anselm was not napping. He was correcting manuscripts in the scriptorium. When the community awoke to go to church for the office of Nones, they heard the signal that someone was dying. Hurrying to the infirmary, they found Anselm embracing his old foe in reconciliation.

The Prior of Bec was solicitous of all the sick and aged. His biographer, Eadmer, tells how the prior cared for Herewald when the only sustenance he could take was the juice from grapes, squeezed one by one into the old monk's mouth by Anselm.

He was a caring instructor in the abbey school, and once reprimanded an abbot of another monastery for the improper treatment of boy students. Parents were still offering their sons as oblations, but in this particular monastery punishment was so extreme that the boys had no chance of normal development.

Anselm was unanimously elected abbot in 1078. His blessing was delayed for six months while he protested his election, and pleaded with the community to choose another monk for their abbot. A chapter meeting was called to deal with the matter of Bec's reluctant abbot-elect. Anselm wept loudly, and prostrating before the monks, begged them to have pity on him. The monks likewise prostrated on the floor of the chapter house, and cried for Anselm to have pity on the abbey. Anselm surrendered. In the fifteen years that he was abbot, he received 122 monks into the community. Among Anselm's letters, there are several to young men whose vocations he encouraged. This was in an age when monasteries did not have to go begging for vocations, but Abbot Anselm took on the role of recruiter. He told young men not to delay their entrance to the monastery. When I was our monastery's vocation director, I once rather timidly asked a young man if he'd like to join us. His reply was, "Hell no."

The Normans had conquered England in 1066, and the monks from Normandy also found their way to the island. Bec made foundations there and it was because of this that Anselm's reputation spread abroad. William II appointed him Archbishop of Canterbury. Anselm resisted this office, too, and the king had to force the crosier into his clenched hand. Like other monks before him who had been elevated to the episcopacy, Anselm had trouble with secular authority. He was exiled twice for defending the church's freedom from royal control. Anselm is renowned for his writings, most notably his mystical theology, and he is called "The Father of Scholasticism." What Aquinas is to the Dominicans, Anselm is to the Benedictines. He died during Holy Week of 1109.

Anselm also left behind a number of prayers and meditations, and a good number of letters. He corresponded with men and women in every station of life. In these letters he reveals a loving relationship with all of them.

Aelred

St. Aelred, the son, grandson, and great-grandson of priests, was born in northern England in 1110. In his early manhood, Aelred was in the service of King David of Scotland. At the age of twenty-four, Aelred heard of a new monastic order that had come to England. These monks observed the Rule of St. Benedict exactly as the lawgiver had intended it to be lived. Soon after visiting the Cistercians at Rievaulx, he asked to enter. In 1142, he became the Abbot of Revesby, and five years later he returned to Rievaulx as its abbot. Like Benedict, Aelred practiced what he preached. This was evident in his Pastoral Prayer: "Teach me therefore, sweet Lord, how to restrain the restless, comfort the discouraged, and support the weak. Teach me to suit myself to everyone according to each one's nature, character, and disposition, as time and place require, in each case, as you would have me do."

Aelred was greatly respected because of his kindness and friendship. Many men were drawn to Rievaulx because of its abbot. At one time the count was six hundred. The monastery was able to make five foundations. Physical suffering was Aelred's cross for the last ten years of his life. His biographer, the monk Walter Daniel, reports that every day twenty or thirty monks visited their ailing and bedridden abbot. "There was nobody to say to them, 'Get out, go away, do not touch the Abbot's bed.' They walked and lay about his bed and talked with him as a little child prattles with his mother."

Bernard's Abbey of Clairvaux founded Rievaulx, and Aelred, because of his writings, preaching, and qualities of leadership, became known as "The Bernard of the North." Bernard himself encouraged Aelred to write *The Mirror of Charity*, a treatise on monasticism. Aelred's other well-known work is *On Spiritual Friendship*. There was a time when reading it was not encouraged in monasteries because Aelred's encouragement of friendship appeared dangerous. My own novitiate class was warned about the forming of an exclusive friendship. Beware of finding yourself with a "p.f.," or personal friend, we were told.

Aelred had a friend, another monk, upon whose death he wrote in *The Mirror of Charity:* "Look at how my own Simon was loved by everyone, embraced by everyone, cherished by everyone! But perhaps some stalwart persons at this moment are passing judgment on my tears, considering my love too human. Let them interpret my tears as they please. But you, Lord, look at them, observe them! Others see what happens outside but do not heed what I suffer within."

The Abbot of Rievaulx wrote of personal friendship, but he did not disassociate himself from the community at large. He may have loved one monk in a special way, but he also loved all of them together. In a homily here one time, a monk of this community told us, "I love you. I love you all very much." Some of the monks were taken aback. One or another even flinched. It seems they had learned the warning about special affections too well, and needed to balance it with a lesson on brotherly love.

Aelred claims man is like an animal if he has no friend in whom to confide. We, however, once had a collie called Katie who functioned as a confidant. I heard someone on a Twelve Step retreat tell another woman, "That dog has heard more Fifth Steps than any other canine." People who came here to do the Fifth Step of Alcoholics Anonymous (Admitting to God, to myself, and to another human being the exact nature of my wrongs) often had a practice run by telling everything to Katie, who listened patiently. "She was such a kind dog," a friend told me after we'd had to put her to sleep. Earlier we had another collie named after Aelred because it is said that a dog is man's best friend.

Heloise and Abelard, and Hildegard, Too

Peter Abelard, a professor of logic at the University of Paris in the twelfth century, was asked by canon Fulbert of Notre Dame Cathedral to tutor his eighteen-year-old niece. Teacher and pupil fell in love, and she became pregnant. Uncle Fulbert was so upset that he had Abelard castrated and banished from the university. What was left for him but to become a monk? He entered the Abbey of St. Denis in Paris. Heloise returned to her family in Brittany, and delivered her baby—a boy. When she went off to become a nun, the child went to live with his father's family. That might have been the end of the story if the two of them hadn't exchanged letters for years afterward.

In one of the letters, Abelard admitted that he was relieved to have been castrated, and to be free from concupiscence. She admitted that life had not become that simple for her. Heloise ruled as the abbess of a monastery founded for her by Abelard. She was well educated in Latin, Greek, and Hebrew. Her nuns ate meat three times a week, drank wine diluted with water, and wore linen lingerie. Abelard continued getting into trouble for the remainder of his life. Threatened with excommunication because of his theological writings and teaching, Abelard retreated to a less prestigious monastery. He died there at the age of sixty-three. Heloise outlived him by another twenty years.

Abbot Peter the Venerable of Cluny admired both of them. He had Abelard's remains transferred from St. Marcel to the

Abbey of the Paraclete, Heloise's monastery. In a letter to her, Peter described Abelard's holy death, and then spoke of their reunion in paradise. He assured Heloise that God was taking good care of her lover and that she and Peter would be reunited for eternity.

In 1187, Abbess St. Hildegard of Bingen incurred an interdict on her abbey for having given burial to a young man who had been excommunicated. She wrote to the Bishop of Mainz, informing him that she and the nuns were refraining from praying the Divine Office in common and from receiving communion. This was done in obedience to the interdict, but with great sadness and bitterness. Furthermore, it was an injustice. Abbess Hildegard, in writing to men, sometimes signed herself "your servant girl," but she never cowered to them. In one letter to an abbot, she likened his behavior to that of both a bear and an ass. She wrote hundreds of letters to ecclesiastical and civil authorities, to monks and nuns and laity.

She is called "the Sibyl of the Rhine" because of her prophecies. Not only was she a prophetess, Hildegard was also a poet, musician, and artist. She wrote a book on medicine, a commentary on St. Benedict's Rule, composed hymns, and illustrated her manuscripts. Her theology was creational, her imagery erotic. She was an ecologist. Hildegard decried the pollution of earth, water, and sky in her day.

By the way, she was exonerated in that matter of the burial in the abbey cemetery. Hildegard knew all along that she was right in showing compassion for the deceased young man and performing a corporal work of mercy.

The Black Plague,
the Reformation, and
Beyond: Hard Times for
Monastic Life in Europe

An Age of Reform

There were restorations of Benedictine monastic ideals, without abandoning the Order, several times before and after the Protestant Reformation. One of them was the Bursfield Union begun in Germany in 1433. It was organized like Cluny. Each monastery had its autonomy, but the Abbot of Bursfield was always the head of the congregation and its visitator. The observance was severe, and the system was pretty well dissipated by 1802.

In 1408, at the failed Cluniac Abbey of St. Justina in Padua, another reform was initiated. A committee appointed abbots of the monasteries affiliated with this congregation. This does not seem very Benedictine, since Benedict preferred that the monks of a given monastery elect their own abbot. The Rhineland mystics found inspiration from this monastic movement. The Justinians also influenced Ignatius of Loyola, who wrote his *Spiritual Exercises* at the Spanish Abbey of Montserrat. The movement lasted only two centuries, and its piety was not particularly Benedictine.

Another reforming Benedictine congregation was the Maurist. Founded in Paris in the seventeenth century, the French Revolution put an end to it. One of the monks, Luc d'Achery, is sometimes called the "Father of Modern Library Science" (or was before the invention of the computer). Another Maurist, Jean Mabillion, wrote *The Annals and Lives of Benedictine Saints*.

Just as Bernard of Clairvaux argued with Benedictine Peter of Cluny, Jean Mabillion tried convincing Armand Jean de Rance, the Trappist Cistercian, of the Maurists' superior merits.

St. Romuald was the founder of the Camaldolese in eleventh-century Italy. This branch of the Benedictine family has endured to this day. The monks and nuns combine the hermetical life with communal monastic life.

Usually reform within a Benedictine monastery can be accomplished without monks leaving to form a new order. A traditional method of checking on a monastery is the periodic visitation. This is conducted by outsiders, and its manner has not changed over the centuries. We have a visitation here every four years. The visitators are an abbot and a monk of other communities. Their purpose is to assess "the way the community of the monastery is achieving its professed purpose." They are also instructed "to correct prudently any abuse which may have arisen either in the spiritual order or in the temporal order."

Most visitations are routine in houses of Benedictine men and women. Although some of the monastics may have complaints about their superior, it's unlikely that any visitator these days hears what was reported in 1442 in an English Cistercian nunnery: The superior had such a fierce temper that she pulled the nuns' hair and called them whores—even when they were all in church. Nor is it likely, as happened in 1228 at an Irish Cistercian monastery, that a recommendation will be made for a monk's transfer to another monastery after he has threatened to kill his own abbot.

All the professed members of the community and the novices have an opportunity to speak with one of the visitators. We are free to express both positive and negative feelings about what it is like in our house. In his opening remarks at one visitation, the Abbot Visitator reminded us that "Listen" is the first word of St. Benedict's Rule. Then he told us to listen carefully to what we ourselves were saying—what we were telling the visitators. This was a request for our honesty. Listen to what you are saying. In your praise of the community, are you being totally honest or are you evading issues that need addressing? In your criticism, are you being totally honest or merely mentioning personal peeves that are of no consequence to the rest of the community?

At the end of a visitation, when the visitators have listened to everyone, they give a report to the community. At one particular visitation they told us, "There are healthy tensions in your life, not all of which are meant to be resolved. Among these are tensions of solitude and community, action and contemplation, asceticism and pastoral activity. Benedictine life has been flexible and able to balance these tensions and needs. You must be open to the future and to changes, to the possibility of new works and ministries. Do not be hung up on living in the past." In other words, we were being told to be aware of the signs of the time, just as our ancestors were in their times.

Not the Best of Times

The Black Plague took its toll on monasteries in the four-teenth century, and the Protestant Reformation in the sixteenth practically wiped out monasticism. Martin Luther, who was an Augustinian friar, had a lot of complaints about the monks and nuns of his day. So did Erasmus, a Dutch priest who stayed in the Church of Rome and made things uncomfortable for it. He said there were monasteries that were hardly any different from public brothels. Luther protested against monastic wealth and comfort. He also had theological objections to monastic life. Monasticism revealed clearly what he meant by faith versus good works. Salvation was found in faith alone, and not in the practices prescribed by monastic rules. Furthermore, monks and nuns were selfish in their pursuit of perfection, and in his day there was enough evidence of their hypocrisy as well.

Monasticism was definitely at low ebb, and a populace who were fed up with monks and nuns heard the voice of Luther. The dissolution of monasteries was inevitable as the Reformation spread throughout Germany. Certainly, not all monastic houses deserved to be suppressed, but in all honesty we have to admit that things really weren't up to snuff in many of them.

Some made a desperate last attempt at reform. Duchess Mechtild tried reforming the community of nuns at Urspring by bringing in nuns from St. Walburga's to give good example to the Urspring nuns. Abbess Barbara von Stein and her followers barricaded themselves in the infirmary with tables and benches set against the door. The duchess ordered an attack, but the noblemen who had accompanied her refused. The nuns, after all, were noblewomen. Mechtild rang the tower bell to call the townspeople. They stormed the monastery and put the resisting nuns under arrest. The St. Walburga nuns took charge, while the Urspring troublemakers departed with their hands tied behind their backs. Some of them did come back, among them a humbled Abbess Barbara von Stein.

When monks and nuns saw the handwriting on the wall, they liberated themselves by simply walking out of the cloister. Luther's future wife, however, had to escape from one by hiding in a barrel that had been emptied of herring. Some convents accepted Lutheranism as a way to keep from being turned out. In those days what opportunities were there for women who left the convent? For some of them not even the offer of a pension if they left and married was appealing. Monastic life for women continued, but with certain modifications. Parts of the Divine Office were eliminated and devotions to the saints and Mary were discouraged. Luther himself, though, had a lifelong devotion to the mother of Jesus.

In some instances, Catholic and Lutheran nuns lived in the same house. When the Abbess of Walrode had to retire in 1538 because of the infirmities of old age, a Lutheran nun replaced her. At Lune in 1526, a Lutheran who had been a Dominican friar was sent by the duke to preach to the Catholic nuns. When the preacher insisted that there were only two sacraments, the abbess left the chapel with eighty-seven nuns following her. They returned with old furs and set them on fire in the sacristy, driving the preacher from the chapel. Most monasteries of men and women passed out of existence because people stopped joining their communities and they simply died out. In fact, Rome closed some monasteries for that reason, and the government confiscated the rest.

Visitation reports in England indicated discipline was on the wane there, too. At Eynsham no one went to common prayer, two women of "doubtful reputation" loitered around the monastery, and the monks were intellectually deprived. The Abbot of Humberstone complained about his monks playing tennis in the village when they should have been in church. Abbot Edmund of Peterborough was accused of seeking too much "solace" in a nearby tavern owned by the abbey. The prior at Ramsey was "a bad-tempered drunk." Only two or three of the forty monks there attended conventual Mass.

King Henry VIII, in 1536, closed monasteries with fewer than thirteen monks or nuns. In 1539, his Act of Suppression closed the rest. In her novel, *The Man on a Donkey,* H.F.M. Prescott relates the demise of an English women's monastery. The last three nuns, one of them being the prioress, were riding toward Richmond and "into the world." "Down at the core of her heart she [the prioress] was angry, though not with the King for turning away all the monks and nuns in England and taking the abbeys into his hand—surely he had a right to them if any had. She was not indeed angry with any man at all, but with God, who had tricked her into thirty years of a nun's life, had suffered her to be Prioress, and to rule, and now had struck power out of her hand."

Some monastic churches became Anglican cathedrals. Others became parish churches with the cloisters falling to ruin or parts of them being used as homes by the local aristocracy. At Durham, Dean William Wittingham's wife used the stone holy water fountain as a kitchen sink, and the tombstones from the monks' cemetery became their sidewalk.

Martin Luther wrote his treatise against monasticism in 1521. Within the year, everyone in his community except the prior had departed from the Augustinian monastery in Wittenberg. Later, when the prior had vacated the building, Luther and his wife, Katherine von Bora, and their large family occupied the monastery. In the next seventy years, 800 out of 1550 monasteries disappeared in Europe. Historian David Knowles, in *Christian Monasticism,* writes: "There were far too many religious houses in existence in view of the widespread decline of the fervent monastic vocation, and . . . in every country the monks possessed too much of wealth and of the sources of production both for their own well-being and for the material good of the economy."

Another English writer, and a monk, Hubert van Zeller laments, in *The Benedictine Ideal*, the loss of Benedictine greats as monasticism went into decline. There was no one of the same stature as Gregory, Boniface, Dunstan, Anselm, and the saintly abbots of Cluny. "There were among the Benedictines no longer the brains which would be able without shame to exchange ideas with Dominican, Franciscan, and, later, Jesuit theologians."

English monasticism went into exile on the continent, with men and women founding monasteries in France and Belgium. By the nineteenth century, they had returned to England as monastic refugees from France—victims of the Revolution. Napoleon continued the suppression of monasteries begun during the French Revolution, and other European governments later imposed restrictions on them.

Monasticism practically disappeared from Europe as it was gaining a foothold in the New World, where the first monastery had been founded in Brazil in 1581. None would be established on this continent until the nineteenth century, although a few children of American colonists did become Benedictines and join European monasteries a hundred years before that. We know of one man and seven women, all Marylanders, who became Benedictines in the eighteenth century. One of them, Rachel Semmes, died in her monastery in Paris on the eve of the French Revolution; her sister Elizabeth also died in Paris, but their sibling, Catherine, made it to England. Marianne Hagan, a nun at Cambrai, was imprisoned for a short time during the Revolution, but she arrived safely in England in 1795 after wandering throughout France. Henrietta Hagan went from France to England with her expelled community, and lived to celebrate the golden jubilee of her profession. Rachel Boone died in England and Elizabeth Rozer in Belgium. Richard Chandler made vows at Douai in France, was ordained in 1710, and died two years later at the age of twenty-seven. These were the first citizens of our land to live under the Rule of St. Benedict. By the time most of them died, independence had come to the country they never saw again. Benjamin Franklin liked visiting the Benedictines in Paris when on diplomatic assignment and may have met more than one monastic from his homeland.

Not all of the young men from Maryland who'd gone abroad to find their religious vocations became Benedictines. John Carroll, the first U.S. citizen to be made a bishop, had become a Jesuit. He was ordained a bishop in England by a Benedictine, Bishop Charles Walmesley, and apparently he liked the Benedictines well enough to invite those in England to make a foundation in western Pennsylvania. They declined. But monks from Bavaria would arrive there in the next century. I've often wondered what Benedictinism in this country would have been like if our roots had been English instead of Germanic.

Monasticism did not fare well in this time of Reformation, Revolution, and religious wars in Europe. However, it never disappeared, and Benedictines continue to hold prominent positions in the church. In 1980, when the Benedictine world observed the 1500th anniversary of St. Benedict's birth, monks and nuns of England gathered at Westminster Cathedral on July 11th, the Feast of St. Benedict. Cardinal Basil Hume, a Benedictine monk, offered Mass for them in his Catholic cathedral. In the afternoon, the monks and nuns walked the length of London's busy Victoria Street to the Church of England's Westminster Abbey to sing Vespers in the magnificent church their ancestors had built—and had lost when monasticism was dissolved in England. A commentator on the ceremony at Westminster Abbey remarked that it was an event "symbolizing both the national and Anglican debt to the Benedictine tradition." He was referring to the manner of worship and the structure of governance for which the Church of England was indebted to the Benedictines, and one of the monks here commented, "In addition to a lot of valuable real estate."

At the Mass in Westminster Cathedral that day, Cardinal Hume told his Benedictine brothers and sisters: "Destroy monasticism in one age, it will appear in another. Drive it out from one nation, it will take root elsewhere. If it dies in one place, it will be reborn somewhere else." Benedictines are like weeds. We keep cropping up, sometimes in the most surprising places. The survivors of Westminster Abbey had fled to France and began English monastic life in exile. During the French Revolution, the English monks returned home and settled at Ampleforth near York. Cardinal Hume was the Abbot of Ampleforth when he was named to the See of Westminster. A descendant of the Westminster monastic community had come back to the old neighborhood.

A Brief History of
Monasticism in
the United States

Welcome to the New World

enedictines have a particular history in the United States. Although ours is a short history, like the history of the country itself, many of the struggles to establish and maintain communities reflect the whole history of Benedictines. Benedictine abbeys in the United States are varied, and reflect the character and charisma of the "saints" that live there. We are all a motley crew. What follows is a brief history, as well as some of my personal experiences and recollections of the Benedictine monastic experiences in The New World.

Boniface Wimmer arrived in Pennsylvania from Bavaria's Metten Abbey with eighteen candidates for monastic life, and only six habits in which to clothe them. His intention was to build a monastery, a school, and a seminary. In 1964, Pope Paul VI named St. Benedict the "Patron and Protector of Europe" because of the influence Benedictines had in Christianizing that continent. When the Benedictines came to the United States in 1846, their purpose was not to convert anyone to Christianity but to preserve the Catholicism of German people like themselves. This would be a center for educating German Americans and a place from which priests could be sent to minister in parishes. In a promotional article written in Germany, Wimmer stated his purpose was not to convert Indians but to save Germans from losing their religious faith if they weren't provided with German-speaking pastors. Wimmer's monks, and the nuns who arrived from Eichstätt six years later, would be missionaries among their own people in a foreign land.

Abbot Boniface Wimmer's community of St. Vincent's at Latrobe grew rapidly. Within ten years his monastery numbered over one hundred members, enabling him to make monastic foundations in other parts of the country. Six separate communities of Benedictine women had been founded by the time Mother Benedicta Riepp died ten years after her arrival in Pennsylvania. There was a revival of Benedictinism in Europe at the same time the order was expanding in the United States. Some European abbots thought that dissatisfied monks would use the missionary calling as an excuse for independence. There was reluctance to send monks and money here. North American foundations received more financial support from King Ludwig of Bavaria than they did from their motherhouses in Europe. The non-supportive attitudes of monks in Europe created in America a sense of self-initiative and even rebellion.

Although these Benedictines lived and worked in a German environment, they were receptive to receiving candidates from other ethnic backgrounds. In fostering support for his venture, Boniface Wimmer called upon the memory of his own patron saint, and the other great Benedictine missionaries who had converted England and Europe. The communities of Beuron, Solesmes, and Maredsous in Germany, France, and Belgium were becoming famous as centers of liturgical worship and scholarship. Of a contemplative bent, these abbeys may have cared for souls in their immediate area, but none of their abbots would have permitted the expansion of parochial work evidenced in this country. Abbot Alexius Edelbrock, the second abbot of St. John's in Collegeville, Minnesota, for example, had monks stationed across the northern part of Dakota Territory in parishes that sprang up along the Northern Pacific Railroad.

Toward the end of his life, in a letter to another American abbot, Boniface Wimmer admitted, "I fear we hold to our Rule too little; therefore God will withdraw His blessing bit by bit

. . . There is too little spirit of the Order, etc. in most of the men . . . The small parishes are the graves of good discipline; we should take them only out of necessity."

Abbot Alexius of St. John's and Mother Scholastica Kerst of the neighboring community of women, St. Benedict's in St. Joseph, were accused of encouraging their subjects to excessive activism. Although the abbey and the Convent of St. Benedict were blessed with numerous vocations from the parishes and schools staffed by the priests and sisters, there was an attitude that increased parochial work detracted from authentic monastic observance. In the meantime, St. John's and St. Benedict's grew to be the two largest communities of Benedictine men and women in the world.

The conflict between monastic observance and apostolic activity increased when American monks began studying in Europe. These young American monks saw the differences in the two expressions of Benedictinism. They became critical of the situation in the United States, opposing activity outside the cloister. James Zilliox, who would become the first American-born abbot, was one of the critics. After his return from Europe, he was disenchanted with monastic life at St. Vincent's, and sought permission to transfer to a European abbey where he could lead a more contemplative kind of life. Abbot Boniface Wimmer refused the request, and named Father James his right-hand man—the prior of St. Vincent's. Behind his abbot's back, Zilliox petitioned Rome for an investigation of what he termed monastic abuses at Latrobe. Nothing came of this, but Zilliox remained rigid in his criticism, even when he appeared to be dying of consumption at the age of thirty-five. When St. Mary's Priory in Newark was raised to an abbey, Wimmer got Zilliox out of his beard by making him abbot of the New Jersey monastery. Abbot James immediately turned over to the diocese several parishes staffed by Benedictines, telling the bishop to staff them with his own priests and not with monks. The new abbot also got rid of the farm outside the city. He resigned after one year because of poor health.

At St. Vincent's he had been novice master upon his return from studies abroad, and now, free of abbatial responsibilities, James Zilliox toured the monasteries founded by St. Vincent's, visiting his former novices, and listening to their complaints about the conditions of American Benedictinism.

Among the Swiss immigrant monks, my community's Benedictine progenitors in this country, there was also an infatuation with European ideals. Some historians now consider the nineteenth-century European revival of monasticism a recapturing of the late Middle Ages instead of a return to the pristine ideals of St. Benedict. In chapter 66 of The Rule, Benedict suggests that a monastery should be self-contained because it is spiritually unhealthy for monks even to go shopping in the world. The Holy Patriarch realized, however, that there were times when monks had to go off the grounds. In chapter 50, he reminds them to say their prayers while traveling and/or working some distance from the monastery. If Benedict's monks and nuns had stayed at home all the time, he would never have become the Patron and Protector of Europe. The Benedictines came to this country in response to pastoral needs, and American bishops readily provided them with parishes and other external works. In the twentieth century, two monasteries were purposely founded in this country to live a type of monastic life that would not include work on the outside. In many ways, they were a return to the original spirit of St. Benedict. Ironically, their founders were two German monks exiled here during World War II.

Benedict says, "Your way of acting should be different from the world's way; the love of Christ must come before all else" (*RB* 4.20-21). Even when Christianity became acceptable and was no longer forced underground, some Christians took flight from the world and went off to live in the desert. They renounced the pleasures of the world in order to follow Christ. They disciplined themselves by not pampering the body and by fasting.

In his own day, Benedict believed that it wasn't good for a monk to go out into the world too often. When I first started out in monastic life, it was called to my attention that I was worldly. When I asked for an explanation, I was informed that it was my use of shampoo and deodorant that was so unmonastic. Even though I was given to a certain amount of pampering of myself, I certainly didn't go out into the world frequently back then. It seems that men and women monastics were once taught to despise the world, and then we were criticized for being naïve and ignorant about the things of the world.

What did Benedict really think of the world? Near the end of his life, he had a vision of the whole world created by God gathered up in something as simple as a single ray of light. We have all been called out of darkness into a wonderful light. In the Prologue, Benedict says, "Let us open our eyes to the light that comes from God" (*RB* Pro. 9). He also advises, "While there is still time, while we are in this body and have time to accomplish things by the light of life—we must run and do now what will profit us forever" (*RB* Pro. 43-44).

Benedict's vision was one of hope and light, even though he lived in a time of darkness and of despair. The Roman Empire had collapsed, and the barbarians had invaded his world. Drought and famine prevailed. Rome was a corrupt city he abandoned in his youth. A community of monks tried poisoning him after asking him to be their abbot. And there was that jealous priest who drove him from Subiaco. Problems existed at Monte Cassino until the end of his life. That's how the world treated Benedict. Yet, he saw the world as clothed in brightness. The world, he knew, was a place redeemed by Christ. No Christian can despise the world for which Christ died. Our calling is to bring light into the dark places of this world. There is a distinct difference between being worldly and apostolic service to the world.

In the beginning, American Benedictines were like Jesus' friends Martha and Mary. In their house a certain amount of tension existed regarding active and contemplative roles. Nevertheless, one supposes these two sisters lived together in mutual dependence and harmony most of the time. Even though Jesus said Mary had chosen the better part, the fact remains that he would never have been served dinner that day if Martha hadn't been toiling away in the kitchen. Our Father Francis, preaching on that gospel text, said, "Jesus would have told Martha, 'You'd better get in there and start rattling those pots and pans.'"

The Swiss Arrive

Our community's European roots are at Einsiedeln Abbey in Switzerland—built on the site where St. Meinrad had his hermitage in the ninth century, and where thieves bludgeoned him to death. Attracted to southern Indiana in 1854 by German settlers, Einsiedeln monks placed the new monastery under the protection of the Swiss saint. The foundation in the United States, in addition to serving the needs of German-speaking immigrants, was also considered a refuge in the event that a government, proving to be unsympathetic to monasteries, might suppress Einsiedeln.

Martin Marty was a student at Einsiedeln when the first two monks departed for Indiana. In a speech he was asked to give at their farewell party, Marty said, "We consider this undertaking to be a return of the Benedictine Order to its original world-historical destiny, expressed most clearly in the beginning." Boniface Wimmer had likewise referred to the past when he was recruiting candidates in Germany for the monastery in Pennsylvania. Marty entered the Abbey of Einsiedeln and was ordained there. Soon afterward he was on his way to St. Meinrad in Indiana, where he was appointed superior with the instructions to either shape up the place or close it down. The Abbot of Einsiedeln wanted him back eventually to be the novice master. But Marty never returned. In 1870, Martin Marty became St. Meinrad's first abbot.

A Swiss priest visiting St. Meinrad's observed that Abbot Martin had little regard for customs, traditions, and bishops. Marty lived in an era when German and Swiss Benedictines, men and women, were forging a religious lifestyle that became distinctly American. He proved to be an innovative abbot. The lay brothers attended the entire Divine Office with the choir monks. A brother candidate was given rank in the community according to the time of his entrance. In 1872, Abbot Martin established a joint novitiate for clerical and non-clerical entrants. He would determine which of them would study for ordination upon the completion of the novitiate. One who had entered as a clerical novice might become a lay brother, and another who had professed as a lay brother might be given theology books to prepare him for ordination. When Martin Marty had his monks abandon the monastic breviary and introduced the use of the Roman breviary, he explained that the former was archaic and that monks shouldn't set themselves apart from the rest of the church. St. Meinrad's was running a seminary where bishops sent their men for training. These future priests were introduced to the Roman Divine Office, but their professors were praying something different. Old World Benedictines were astounded. Placidus Wolter at Beuron in Germany berated Marty in a letter he circulated throughout Europe. He referred to "the American choir" and "the dreadful democracy and mania for wiping out all class distinction." Not all the monks in his own house appreciated Marty's controversial practices.

Martin Marty's career as abbot, however, was drawing to an end. St. Meinrad's Abbey was asked to financially support the newly organized Catholic Indian Missionary Association. This request prompted a generous personal response from Marty, who in 1876 went to the Standing Rock Reservation in Dakota Territory where he examined the possibilities of mission work, and the founding of a monastery. This was the manner in which the tribes of Europe had been converted to Christianity, and Marty was convinced that a stable monastic community, praying and working, would affect the same result on the North American Continent.

Back in Indiana, his monastic community was beginning to show some concern about the abbot. Announcement of his departure for Dakota Territory had not been made until the evening before he left. Not even his council knew of his intention, and now he'd been absent from the monastery far too long. He would never return to it as its abbot. In 1879, Rome named him Vicar Apostolic of the whole Dakota Territory. Our nation was a century old when Martin Marty arrived in these parts, but North and South Dakota had not yet become states. He and the other Benedictines he brought to this region would play a significant part in the religious development of what are now the two Dakotas. Marty was a zealous missionary among the Indian people, and willingly embraced all the hardships of life on the prairie, traveling great distances on horseback to visit Indian camps. As Vicar Apostolic, he was the head shepherd of all people—Indian and white—who lived in the territory. He established his headquarters in Yankton, the territorial capital. Soon Benedictine sisters from Switzerland moved to Yankton.

Martin Marty was a contradictory character. Beneath his humble exterior there was an autocrat who crept out occasionally and entered into conflict with his subjects. Today we would call him a controller. He interfered where he shouldn't have. Father Isidor Hobi confronted his abbot about changes that had been made at St. Meinrad, pointing out that they violated canon law. The old priest showed him the decree he copied into his notebook—"*in meinem Buchle*" (in my little notebook). Abbot Martin confiscated the priest's notebook, saying that he himself was now the law. He was such a meddler in the lives of the Yankton sisters that he changed assignments made by the prioress, and so paternalistic toward them that he often assumed the responsibility of doing their shopping, even to the procurement of their shoes.

Martin Marty did not remain in Dakota. He became the Bishop of St. Cloud, Minnesota, and died there in 1896. Shortly before his death, he traveled back to Dakota for the Catholic Indian Congress, and was graciously welcomed by his Dakota friends who had named him *Sinasopa Itonca Tamahetscha* (Black Robe Lean Chief). St. Meinrad's Abbey retained his concern for the Indian people and over the years established four centers in the two Dakotas. The monastery he had envisioned was not founded until 1950. Our community at Blue Cloud Abbey is the fulfillment of that dream.

Frowin Conrad, the Swiss-born Abbot of Conception Abbey in Missouri, could not go along with some of Martin Marty's ideas. He corresponded with the Wolter brothers in Europe, complaining about Marty to these two Benedictine siblings, one of whom, Maurus, was the Abbot of Beuron, and the other, Placidus, who became the Abbot of Maredsous. Placidus once remarked, "One may expect that in a nation which is so young, and which has been compounded from such diversified elements as the American nation undoubtedly is, that changes and novelties will be embraced all too freely. They are altogether too bold in changing laws, regulations, customs, and institutions to fit the needs of the moment, and in adjusting themselves to times and places, rather than in making the latter conform to the former." This does not reflect Pope Gregory's attitude regarding Augustine's mission to England near the end of the sixth century. Gregory told Augustine to practice adaptation in a new land, to make use of what he found there.

Regardless of what European Benedictines thought, things had to be different in America. When Marty the Indian missionary became Vicar Apostolic of Dakota Territory, the monks and nuns he brought to this land would not be strictly confined to their cloisters. They would work in parishes, schools, hospitals, and on Indian reservations. There would always be some negative reaction from the monks and nuns to these external works. Often the men and women successors of the pioneer superiors tried reforming their communities by making them more enclosed, but American Benedictinism had already set out on a different course.

Vital, Ildephonse, and Felix

During the first half of the twentieth century, American monasteries were still receiving small numbers of German-speaking men and women. Brother Vital, Father Ildephonse, and Brother Felix came to this South Dakota monastery by way of our mother abbey in Indiana. Brother Vital, born in Salzburg, was our eldest community member for a long time. He liked to pretend regret at every birthday beyond the age of eighty. When Brother Alexius, his younger confrere by five years, died before him, Brother Vital commented, "The trouble with this place is that no one dies in seniority."

As a young man, he learned cabinetmaking and excelled in this craft until he became crippled by arthritis in his old age. When he was in his late twenties he left Austria and entered the Abbey of St. Andre in Belgium. The Benedictine monasteries in his homeland were not engaged in missionary work, but St. Andre was. He dreamed of going to Africa or China, but war broke out the first week he was in the monastery. In 1914, Vital was indeed an alien in a foreign land. He had to leave Belgium. Soon after his return to Austria he was drafted into the army. Sent to the front, he was promptly taken prisoner, and spent the remainder of the First World War in Russia. His talent was employed in making skis for the captors.

After the war Vital came to the United States. The abbot of St. Meinrad's Abbey had gone to Europe recruiting young men for the brotherhood. A good number of them, mostly from Germany, responded. His desire to go to the missions was fulfilled with an assignment to St. Michael's Indian Mission in North Dakota. For thirty years, he practiced his trade there. With the founding of Blue Cloud Abbey in 1950, he built our first choir stalls in the carpenter shop at St. Michael and also a vestment case that is still in use here at the abbey.

In 1964 he retired to the abbey. The Indian children were especially sad to have him leave the reservation. He could always be interrupted in the carpenter shop to make things or do repairs for them. He worked faithfully in our library until he became bedridden several months before his death at the age of eighty-six. Besides being afflicted with arthritis, he was a diabetic and had a heart condition. Nevertheless, he had great stamina. In the summer he could walk a mile supported by two canes.

Brother Vital was an avid reader, and received many books and periodicals from relatives in Austria. Once when I took a meal to him in his room, he pointed to the book on his desk. "Ach, that book!" he said. "I read it at night and when I go to sleep, I have bad dreams." It was a history of the Habsburgs.

At the age of twenty, Father Ildephonse came to this country from that part of Germany known as Swabia. He professed vows at St. Meinrad's two months into World War I, and was ordained to the priesthood the same month the Treaty of Versailles was signed. Had he remained in Europe, his studies would no doubt have been delayed by military conscription.

He had been the superior at St. Michael's Indian Mission for ten years by the time our monastery was founded in 1950. Brother Vital stayed at the mission and built the choir stalls for the new monastery, but Father Ildephonse was brought here to raise funds for the construction project. He knew the right people, some of whom organized an annual Cadillac Dinner. The diners paid over a hundred dollars per plate, and one of them won a new Cadillac at the end of the meal. Father Ildephonse was always present for this event in Minneapolis. A wealthy benefactor and friend of Father Ildephonse gave us a Cadillac one time. I'm sure Father Ildephonse must have discouraged her from doing this, but the chauffeur drove it here from Minneapolis—and then drove it back when the abbot said it would be unseemly for monks to be driving around in a Cadillac.

The only time I ever saw Father Ildephonse upset was when a prank was played on him in the refectory. At breakfast one of the monks had put a sliced grapefruit on Father Ildephonse's chair, and he sat on it. That morning silence was broken in the refectory.

For the last five years of his life, he was deaf and unable to speak coherently as the result of a stroke. He gracefully accepted this burden, but was still eager to work. He went to the library every day. Whenever a member of the community would drop by to see him after he'd taken to remaining in his room, Father Ildephonse extended a firm handshake, a gracious smile, and a delightful laugh. Then he would speak gibberish, although the final words were often discernibly German.

Brother Felix, a Bavarian, was also stationed at St. Michael's Mission. His assignment was the result of having told off the abbot at St. Meinrad's. Brother Felix ran the poultry farm there. One day the abbot was out for a walk and got caught in a rainstorm. He sought shelter in the chicken house. While he had him as a captive, Brother Felix let the abbot know exactly what was wrong with the abbey and its administration. Soon after this, Brother Felix was on his way to North Dakota. He and Father Ildephonse both came to Blue Cloud in 1950. When Father Ildephonse went about the country soliciting funds from benefactors for the construction of our monastery, Brother Felix was his chauffeur. Although I saw Father Ildephonse upset only once, I often saw Brother Felix lose his temper.

He had a space all his own where he tended to the mail and answered the telephone. We cautiously entered it, knowing the limits of how far we could go. "You got no right in here!" he would shout if we trespassed. We called the place "Felix's bunker." He once kicked out a visiting bishop.

The Sisters

Women have been part of American Benedictine history from its beginnings. Abbot Boniface Wimmer brought the first Benedictine women to this country. Arriving in 1852 at St. Mary's, Pennsylvania, from Eichstätt in Bavaria, the sisters had come to assist the monks in caring for German immigrants. Wimmer wanted them under his control, so he and Mother Benedicta Riepp had disagreements from the beginning. In 1859 she wrote a letter to a Roman Cardinal detailing the conflict with the Patriarch of American Benedictines. She asked the Vatican official to agree with her statement that matters pertaining to religious women should not always be decided by men.

Wimmer lost out, but so did she. American Benedictine women were placed under the authority of bishops, who meddled just as much as Boniface Wimmer had. Bishops presided at the election of superiors, received the profession of the sisters' vows, and often determined who would enter the communities and who should not. Benedictine women in the United States were not strictly enclosed, and because of this they were no longer considered nuns. Nuns, according to ecclesiastical law of the time, were cloistered. Other women bound by religious vows were called sisters. Sister Judith Sutera, in *True Daughters: Monastic Identity and American Benedictine Women's History*, writes: "If they had succumbed to pressure from those who told them that they could not do what they knew they could or call themselves what they knew they were, the institution of Benedictinism among American women would have been severely limited. Rather, they continued to negotiate on points which they had been told were not negotiable. They took the time and the extraordinary effort to keep ironing out their difficulties rather than settle for mediocre or quick solutions."

Most of us who live in Dakota monasteries owe a great deal of gratitude to the Swiss Benedictines. When the Territory was divided into two states, Martin Marty became the first bishop of what is now the Diocese of Sioux Falls. In 1889, Bishop Marty brought Benedictine sisters from Melchtal in Switzerland to the Black Hills of Dakota. They settled in Sturgis, opening St. Martin's Academy soon after their arrival. Calamity Jane's daughter was a student of theirs for a while. In 1962, the sisters moved to Rapid City. Among the graves of the townspeople with whom the pioneer sisters are buried in Sturgis is that of Poker Alice, who was the most famous woman gambler of the American West.

The Benedictine Sisters of Sacred Heart Monastery in Yankton, South Dakota, originate from Maria Rickenbach by way of Maryville, Missouri. A group of sisters broke off from the Missouri convent and moved to Dakota in 1883. In 1906, the Yankton sisters established a permanent recruiting center at Einsiedeln for Swiss women who wished to enter the South Dakota community. The aspirants were taught English at Einsiedeln, and they assisted the monks in caring for pilgrims. During World War I there was a shortage of food, and the government urged the growing of large gardens. The monks had the young women working in theirs. The building across the street from the monastery that housed these future religious women is now a hotel. World War II prevented the flow of vocations to the United States. But from the beginning of the century until the 1930s, many Swiss women, and some Germans, came to South Dakota to become Benedictine sisters. Mother of God Monastery near us in Watertown is a daughter house of the Yankton community. We monks were invited there for a 4th of July picnic, and I was eating with several of the older sisters, one of whom had a German accent. I asked if she had come from Switzerland or Germany. She was from Strasburg, North Dakota—Lawrence Welk's hometown.

Benedictine women have flourished in the United States. One hundred and fifty years after the arrival of Mother Benedicta Reipp and the first Benedictine sisters in the United States, forty-six monasteries of women could trace their origins to them. Among these are houses in Canada, Mexico, Puerto Rico, Bahamas, Taiwan, and Japan.

Over the Alps at Grandma's House

*A*utonomy is something for which every Benedictine community strives. Independence from the motherhouse is the future goal of every new monastery that is founded. Most monasteries—men's and women's—are nevertheless united in a congregation, and are expected to adhere to a particular constitution and statutes. All of the monks in our congregation have the common identity of Old Word origins at either Einsiedeln or Engelberg Abbeys in Switzerland. Having this common denominator, however, does not mean that we are uniform in everything else. There is a great amount of diversity in the Swiss American Congregation. (A monk of another congregation once told me, "Yours sounds like the brand name of a cheese.") Some of the monasteries in our congregation operate seminaries; others run high schools. Most of them have facilities for retreats. For some communities, running a retreat house is their exclusive work. Three of the monasteries have made foundations in Guatemala and one in Mexico. Several of the monasteries have presses, two of them are widely known because of their mail order business. The liturgy is celebrated in the vernacular at all monasteries save two, where Latin is used.

Vincent Wehrle was an Einsiedeln monk who found his way to Dakota and an Indian mission staffed by the monks from St. Meinrad. He wanted to found a monastery, and eventually he was allowed to do so, although his monastic community was reluctant to become involved. Writing to Wehrle at Devils Lake, in what is now North Dakota, the Swiss abbot told him: "Monks are of flesh and blood and can be pardoned for not finding an attraction to a place of vast prairies where there are no trees and terrible winters with their more terrible storms." Wehrle shouldn't have written home about the weather conditions in Dakota. He was determined to make something of his venture, though, and in 1899 his little community of St. Gall's Priory transferred to Richardton in the western part of the state, where it is now known as Assumption Abbey. Wehrle became the community's first abbot. In 1910, he was named the first bishop of Bismarck and for several years he functioned as both abbot and bishop.

The monasteries in this country with an Einsiedeln connection all have a statue of the Black Madonna in their churches. Pilgrimages to Einsiedeln began in the twelfth century and continue to this day. It is one of the prominent Marian shrines of Europe. Pilgrims venerate Mary by praying before a statue of her holding the Christ child. The present statue was carved in 1466. Mary's face and hands and the naked child have turned black from the smoke of the candles that the countless pilgrims have placed before the statue. Unlike the Swiss, we do not adorn our statue with real clothing and jewelry. In Switzerland she wears a brocade gown, a crown, and earrings. Construction of the present monastery buildings and church, designed by one of the monks, was completed in 1719. The Abbey of Einsiedeln is a superb example of Baroque architecture. None of the monasteries founded in the New World bore any resemblance to the mother abbey.

Whenever Blue Cloud monks are fortunate to be traveling in Europe, we make an effort to stop at Einsiedeln. I have been there twice. The first time I was in the company of my confrere Father Wilfrid and Brother Placid of Assumption Abbey. We arrived on October 4th, and there was snow in the mountains and on the ground. Abbot Georg and the guest master, Father Wolfgang, had visited both of our monasteries two years previously. They had come to United States for the centenary celebration of Subiaco Abbey in Arkansas, and had visited the other communities with whom Einsiedeln is related. Although the Swiss monks had invited us Americans to visit them, the guest master was surprised when three of us showed up unannounced. Another monk from North America arrived without reservations the same day that we did. He was from St. Benoit du Lac in Quebec.

The Swiss, with their penchant for precise time, like having things done on schedule. In the first place, they prefer that appointments be made ahead of time and then kept. Other monks from my community have also gone to Einsiedeln without writing ahead, and were unable to get into the monastery. Of course they went about it all wrong. Instead of going to the porter's office and announcing themselves, they tried entering the monastery from the church. Not wearing habits and unable to communicate in German, they were driven from the cloister by Einsiedeln monks who presumed they were tourists or pilgrims who had wandered out of bounds.

My companions and I were graciously received. After the guest master had recovered from his shock at seeing us, we were given the grand tour. One of the highlights was the viewing of many illuminated medieval manuscripts in the library. Two of the English-speaking monks proudly escorted us through the new school building. One of them was the science teacher, and when I saw all the modern equipment in his laboratory, I thought it was quite a contrast with the Baroque. There was another area in the school that was distinctly different. The boys' recreation room was done up in American cowboy motif and called The Saloon. The students drank soda pop and ate potato chips at the bar.

At Vespers, I was a bit nervous about the procession from the choir stalls to the shrine of the Black Madonna near the entrance of the church. The monks process there every day while singing the Magnificat. Years ago I'd heard about this procession, but I never thought I'd be in it. We were told to keep in step and sway with the monks in the right direction. A monk from St. Meinrad's had once been kicked out of the procession because he couldn't catch on. It wasn't all that difficult. It was something like a slow snake dance around the homecoming bonfire of my high school days.

Security is tight at Einsiedeln because of the many strangers who are around all the time. The guest master gave us a key to the front door in case we wanted to go out for the evening. But the instructions for using it seemed complicated, so we decided not to risk being locked outside the monastery. It was already complicated enough being locked up inside the monastery. We were staying in the guest quarters, and had always been accompanied in and out of the cloister by a monk who unlocked doors. In the morning, I got into the refectory by following the monks. After I'd eaten breakfast, wondering all the time where Wilfrid and Placid were, I tried to go back to my room. But I was locked in the cloister and had to wait for a local monk to release me. Abbot Georg and my traveling companions were waiting for me to eat breakfast with them in the guest dining room. I suffered the embarrassment of eating two breakfasts.

What did I make of Einsiedeln on that first visit? Was it like going home? The story is told of an abbot from there who visited the American daughter monastery some years back—close to a hundred years after its founding. The Indiana abbot informed the visitor from abroad about all of the motherhouse customs that were still observed in the New World. The Swiss abbot was amazed, since many of those customs had been abandoned long ago at Einsiedeln. I can recall a custom that was brought to our monastery from St. Meinrad's by way of Switzerland. On Christmas Eve, we were awakened for Midnight Mass by the angels' song. The abbey schola passed through the corridors singing a lovely Einsiedeln melody. Now that is gone. We don't even have to go to bed before Midnight Mass.

Our roots are at Einsiedeln. Roots are deep in the soil, but traditions are like leaves that fall off a plant. Of course, some traditions and customs need to be retained for the health of the plant. A monastery cannot shed all of its traditions. If all the leaves fall off, the plant is dead. Some customs from St. Meinrad's that were established in the early history of my monastery are no longer observed. Meanwhile, we have formed our own traditions.

When Einsiedeln monks were planting roots in American soil, the Germans were reviving Benedictinism at Beuron. How different the two were. For the Beuronese Congregation, Gregorian chant was strictly plainchant. At Einsiedeln and other Swiss abbeys, Italian provenance had found its way into the chant. Beuronese churches were artistic but simple. Swiss Baroque churches looked like orchestra halls.

My second visit to our grandmother abbey was with Brother Sebastian and a tour group of thirty, most of them Oblates of St. Benedict associated with our monastery. On the flight over with Swissair, I met a wrestling coach from Glarus, Switzerland. He'd taken his Swiss wrestling team to New Glarus, Wisconsin. When I told him we were going to Einsiedeln, he said, "Ah, you are attending *The Great Theater of the World*." He was referring to Calderon's morality play, performed every five years by the townspeople. We did not attend the play, but we saw the stage and bleachers erected for it in front of the abbey. On our first night in Einsiedeln, some of us watched the angels on their way to the performance. They had put on their costumes at the schoolhouse, about a block from the abbey—men and women, boys and girls, all in colorful robes and elegant wings. Some of the angels were carrying musical instruments, while some of the teenage angels had boom boxes tuned to their ears. That did not seem particularly Baroque.

A Swiss Monk Who Stayed at Home

There was another Meinrad at Einsiedeln besides the ninth-century martyr saint upon whose grave the monastery was built. Although this Meinrad isn't officially recognized as a saint, his cause for that honor was introduced in the 1940s. It doesn't seem to have gone anywhere.

Brother Meinrad was born in 1848, the tenth of twelve children. Two siblings born after him died in infancy. His father was a schoolteacher and the owner of a small farm on which the family lived. Education was made available to his older brothers, one of whom became a priest. But Gebhard, which was Meinrad's baptismal name, was unable to go to high school because his father was having financial problems. At the end of primary school, Gebhard went to work in a factory. At the age of sixteen, he became a tailor's apprentice. He was working at that trade when he decided to enter the monastic life.

By then Einsiedeln had made its foundation in the United States, a place of sanctuary if the Swiss government should begin suppressing monasteries. The Jesuits had already been driven out of Switzerland. Gebhard Eugster expressed his willingness to go to America, but the need never arose. He remained at Einsiedeln in the tailor shop for the rest of his life. He died in 1925, the year of his golden jubilee of profession, at the age of seventy-seven.

Brother Meinrad's life portrays the good zeal St. Benedict wants his followers to practice. "This, then, is the good zeal which monks must foster with fervent love: *They should each try to be the first to show respect to the other* [Rom 12:10], supporting with the greatest patience one another's weaknesses of body or behavior" (*RB* 72.3-5). For many years, Brother Meinrad, rising early from sleep, served Mass for a cranky priest. St. Benedict admonishes the monk not to pursue "what he judges better for himself, but instead, what he judges better for someone else" (*RB* 72.7). For a time, Brother Meinrad was in charge of the vestry. He distributed new clothing to his confreres, but kept the used clothing for himself. Although he willingly submitted to every command given him and never questioned it, he was known to go to bat for fellow monks when he felt they were being treated unfairly. And whenever he saw the need, he spoke out on behalf of the lay employees at Einsiedeln.

He was a model of simplicity and docility. He had a reputation for being kind and patient. On the other hand, he annoyed some of the monks by his groaning and sighing while at prayer and reading. He had a temper that flared up occasionally. Sometimes his workmanship was hindered by haste. Clutter often took over his vestry. He was human enough to admit that carnal thoughts plagued him now and then, even in his old age. The saintly, after all, are human.

Brother Meinrad liked playing cards—and winning. He enjoyed climbing the Alps, and vacationing with the monks at Lake Zurich. There were pleasures in his life. Nevertheless, fun had its limits. He was a stickler for discipline. Once when he and some brothers were on a walk, they came to the home of a relative of one of them. She invited them in for lunch. Brother Meinrad, adhering to chapter 51 of The Rule, refused to take a meal outside the monastery. In wintertime, the other monks covered their heads when they were in the unheated church, but Brother Meinrad never put up his hood. In the tailor shop, his fingers became numb from the cold, but he did not linger at warming his hands over the stove. He scorned comforts and sought out inconveniences, even to the point of sitting on a chair without leaning back. He loved food but ate sparingly. His confreres joked that Gebhard Eugster would willing indulge, but Brother Meinrad was abstemious.

He suffered colds all winter long. No doubt his constant coughing was another source of annoyance for the monks as they paid the price of living with a saint. In 1896, he almost died of pneumonia. From that time on his health was in steady decline. His desire to do more fasting was realized when a stomach ailment, brought on by fasting, made it impossible for him to eat solid foods the rest of his life. Although he wanted to wear a hair shirt, his confessor forbade it.

Brother Meinrad revealed to a Trappist brother, a World War I refugee living at Einsiedeln, that he himself had been thinking about becoming a Trappist because they were more penitential than Benedictines. He seems to have succeeded fairly well in living a penitential life at Einsiedeln. Candidates for sainthood are described as having been imbued with heroic virtue. Although Benedict outlined a life of moderation—"nothing harsh, nothing burdensome," some souls always catch fire and burn up.

The First Benedictine Abbot of
the Church of England

Although most American abbeys trace their roots to Swiss and German Benedictines, the Anglican Benedictines also have a strong presence in the United States. In the twentieth century, one British Benedictine stands out as a particularly colorful member of the motley crew. Benjamin Carlyle, a medical student was, like Benedict, a school dropout who embraced monastic life. Benjamin founded a community of Anglican monks, and became their Abbot Aelred. His community changed locations several times before 1906, when it settled off the coast of Wales on the Isle of Caldy, where a permanent and grandiose monastery was constructed. These monks attempted to interpret The Rule of Benedict literally, yet they assumed some of the monastic trappings of the later Middle Ages that didn't seem in keeping with St. Benedict's ideals. This, of course, had happened on other occasions in monastic history.

The Church of England looked upon them as misguided romantics. While Aelred Carlyle desperately sought approval from the hierarchy, he also tended to ignore authority when it benefited his cause. Life at Caldy had its strictness. The monks ate no meat and kept a Trappist schedule: early to bed and early to rise. On Friday mornings, each monk applied the discipline to himself. This meant fifty to sixty lashes on his bare back while reciting the *Miserere*. Still, there was time for frivolity. Monsignor Ronald Knox remembered visiting Caldy on a summer's afternoon, and finding the community at the beach in the buff, all except Brother Anselm, a fully clothed Victorian gentleman. Peter Anson, a former monk of Caldy, in *Abbot Extraordinary*, his biography of Aelred Carlyle, recalled, "Visitors were sometimes surprised at this display of monastic nudity, and it embarrassed not a few shy postulants to find that a vocation to the monastic life included this sideline."

Aelred Carlyle was a most unconventional abbot in his time and place. Anglican ecclesiastics were usually shocked by his familiarity with the monks. St. Benedict, also, would probably have been shocked. He said we weren't to use nicknames, but Abbot Aelred used them all the time for the monks of Caldy. Among the nicknames were: Gubs, Bobby, and Old Wilf. Peter Anson became Beloved "because one day when reading in the refectory, I stammered over this word which was repeated at intervals in the life of some saint. My Abbot, getting very impatient, shouted from his table in the far corner facing the reading desk, 'Oh! Shut up, Beloved, and come down.'"

In 1913, Aelred Carlyle and most of his monks entered the Church of Rome. In 1928, the community moved to Prinknash in England where it remains to this day. The building the monks lived in for many years had once been a summer home for the abbots of Gloucester. The last of them entertained Henry VIII and Anne Boleyn there when they were all still on friendly terms. The monks of Prinknash are known for their practice of various arts and crafts, a tradition inherited from their Anglican founders who produced vestments, embroidery, wood carvings, sandals, and metal works ranging from chalices to cigarette boxes and jewelry. Trappists from Belgium settled on the Isle of Caldy a year after the Benedictines left it. Today these monks earn their livelihood by making perfume.

Aelred Carlyle left the Benedictines and became a diocesan priest in British Columbia, working among the indigenous people, seamen, prisoners, and the down-and-out on the streets. For a brief time, he tried his vocation with the Carthusian hermits in Spain and then returned to Canada. After an absence of thirty years, he returned to Prinknash and became a Benedictine again. He died there in 1955 at the age of eighty-one.

Some years ago, I spent Christmas at Prinknash Abbey. When Aelred Carlyle founded his community, he gave the monks a white habit—and white is worn to this day. I was the black sheep in the fold. Upon my arrival, the old retired Abbot Dyfrig came to my room. A little confused, he presumed I'd come to Prinknash in the capacity of a visitator. He asked if I'd like to look at the financial records. I assured him that wouldn't be necessary, and we sat down to a pleasant conversation.

On Christmas morning, the monks were given their mail that had collected throughout Advent, and the television set was brought out. Viewing the *telly* was allowed only on Christmas and Easter, as was smoking—so cigarettes and cigars were passed around. Through a haze that afternoon, I watched, much to my surprise, *Dallas*. I hadn't expected to spend Christmas in an English monastery with J.R. and all the other Ewings.

Father Michael, who was in his nineties, met me in the corridor just after the Queen had presented her Christmas message on television. He'd missed it again. "I always aim to watch the Queen, but I never get there on time." I had missed her too.

The old monastery was known as St. Peter's Grange, and was used as a retreat house, but today the monks are living in it once again. As it occurs in so many places these days, the building constructed in 1970 had become too large for the few monks left.

Father Denys Prideaux, an Anglican Benedictine who did not go over to Rome with the rest of the Caldy community, established monastic life back in England. It was from this Nashdom Abbey that St. Gregory's Abbey at Three Rivers, Michigan, was founded in 1939. A priest of the Episcopal Church and a few other Americans had gone to England in 1935 in order to become

Benedictines. Returning to the United States, they were in Valparaiso, Indiana, before moving to Michigan in 1946. Nashdom Abbey relocated in 1987, and is now known as Elmore Abbey.

There are Anglican Benedictine monasteries of women as well as men in England. Lutheran men and women have monasteries in Europe nowadays, and there is a small monastery for men in Oxford, Michigan—just down the road from a Catholic Benedictine monastery. Several of the orders in the Episcopal Church identify as Benedictine in spirit. The International Congress of Benedictine Abbots, convened in Rome in 1966, made this declaration: "Anglican, Lutheran, and Reformed monks and nuns are to be considered and treated as true brothers and sisters of our Holy Father Benedict."

A Benedictine Beginning

Our Father Tim always said he was opposed to the founding of Blue Cloud Abbey. In October of 1949, Abbot Ignatius Esser traveled from Indiana to meet with the monks from St. Meinrad's who were stationed on four Indian reservations in the two Dakotas. The abbot wanted to discuss the proposed monastery that had been talked about for years. If it were started, the present missionaries would become members, and all future missionaries would come from the Dakota monastery. Father Tim suggested that Abbot Ignatius look for some other place in which to found a monastery. He told him that the missionaries were doing just fine without having a monastery in their backyard.

In 1887, when Father Vincent Werhle was assigned to Immaculate Conception Mission at Stephan, Dakota Territory, Bishop Martin Marty told him, "Stephan is intended as a location of the Benedictine house, which we hope to see flourishing in the course of the next fifteen years and enter the twentieth century as an abbey." Establishing that Benedictine house had been delayed long enough. It was only getting started by the middle of the twentieth century.

Even before the St. Meinrad monks had voted to make a foundation, Abbot Ignatius had been out scouting for a site. On his return from the meeting with the Dakota missionaries, Abbot Ignatius saw the hill upon which our abbey now stands.

111

He recorded in his journal: "I was driving westward on Federal Highway 12 in the region near Marvin. Brother Meinrad, my traveling companion, turned to look back toward his rear right. He let out an exclamation that induced me to pull off to the side of the road, and enjoy the scene with him. It was truly gratifying." They were looking at the Whetstone Valley. Abbot Ignatius saw it as "a sequestered spot, ideal for recollection or the secluded life." The property was purchased. In the spring of 1950 the monks already in the missions became members of the new community, and twenty more arrived from Indiana to construct the monastery building and pray the Divine Office, the work to which St. Benedict says nothing else should be preferred.

Abbot Ignatius, always careful about details, listed the many jobs that would occupy the monks in the new monastery. In addition to the superiors—abbot, prior, and subprior—there would be council members, house confessors, a treasurer, procurator, novice master, infirmarian, vestiarius, house prefect, building master, master of ceremonies, director of chant and the schola, organist, archivist, chronicler, librarian, farm superintendent, porter, sacristan, tailor, cook, baker, photographer, mechanic, butcher, barber, shoemaker, and carpenter. "This will keep just about everybody busy," he said.

"Founding Day will be open to the public," Abbot Ignatius declared. "We really expect to see a great gathering on what used to be Oscar Kasperson's land. The Most Reverend Bishop Brady will grace the event by his presence. . . . And general notices in the newspapers will invite the local public. We want all around to rejoice with us on this great occasion, and we should show hospitality in line with St. Benedict's beautiful teaching in the Holy Rule.

"There will be a big lunch stand well supplied with buns and bread and hamburger meat and hot dogs and coffee and soft drinks and even ice water. As long as it lasts, food and drink will be served gratis to all who call at the lunch counter. St. Benedict says: 'Let all the guests arriving at the monastery be received as

Christ himself.' We are not going to charge Christ fifteen cents for a hamburger and a nickel for a soft drink." Can anyone remember if a hamburger cost only fifteen cents in the 1950s?

Abbot Ignatius was deceased by the time the community celebrated its golden jubilee, and so were half of the forty monks he had appointed to start the monastery. A few years ago, someone in the community pondered whether or not there would be any monks left here by the turn of the century. We're still here, but our numbers are much smaller than when we began in 1950. A friend of mine visited St. Aelred's burial site at Rievaulx in England. "What an amazing place that still is," he said. "What a magnificent monastic house it must have been." Although there is no comparison of our architecture with that of twelfth-century Cistercian Rievaulx, people may say the same thing about our abbey if it's in a state of ruin a hundred years from now.

Unlike St. Benedict, who had a vision of Monte Cassino's destruction by the Lombards, we just don't know the future of our abbey. Benedict, knowing that everything he had built at Monte Cassino would fall into the hands of the barbarians only thirty years after his death, got on with the realities of present day life. He and his followers didn't brood over the future. A few years ago, a newly arrived candidate often asked visitors and us, "What do think Blue Cloud's future is?" He left here with this matter unresolved.

A sociology class from a nearby college used to come here every year on a tour of intentional communities. Some of their questions were very surprising to us. "Do you think you guys will ever get married?" They had just come from a Hutterite colony, where the members of that community are given to marriage. Marriage, of course, has contributed to the propagation of their intentional community. I'm confident, however, that marriage will never be our intention in this commune.

"What do you think Blue Cloud Abbey will be like in thirty years?" a student asked. "Or do you think it will still be around?" The question is comparable to asking a recovering alcoholic, "Do you think you'll still be sober in thirty years?" For the alcoholic staying sober is a daily occupation. One can't live in the past, and the future is not yet here. St. Benedict says we "must run and do now what will profit us forever" (*RB* Pro. 44). Now means today. This reminds me of Brother Gene who, while suffering with cancer, tended roses in the greenhouse practically every day until he was confined to bed the week before his death.

While we have light, we work with the tools that St. Benedict has given us until the end of our lives. For my sixty-fifth birthday, I received a Medicare card and my first Social Security check. Actually, I didn't even see the check. It was delivered directly to the treasury. These days when vocations are so scarce in this hemisphere, some of us will continue being counted as younger members of our communities even after the age of sixty-five.

Nevertheless, time passes and we all age physically. But do we mature spiritually? We make spiritual progress in our lifetime, but having reached a particular age is no guarantee that we have ascended to the heights of perfection. Abba Moses, one of the old time desert monks, warned against the advice of men "of whom white hair and length of years are the sole recommendation." Benedict also realized that not all old men are reliable. He wanted a "sensible" old man to function as the monastery's porter (*RB* 66.80). I like Abbot David Parry's comment on this: "Not any old fool will do."

Abba Moses cited laziness as the reason why certain monks never develop spiritually. Abbot Benedict addressed sloth in the very Prologue of his Rule, and told us to get moving. In fact, he told us we should be running. In the last chapter, he asked, "Are you hastening toward your heavenly home? Then with Christ's help, keep this little rule that we have written for beginners" (*RB* 73.8). I realize that now my journey is coming closer to its end.

A Benedictine Pilgrimage

It was raining that day in December 1980 when the thirteen of us who were in a three-month study program at Sant'Anselmo, the Benedictines' international college in Rome, went to Norcia. Ours was certainly a motley crew. We were attending lectures presented in English, but it was not the first language of everyone in the group. A Swiss Benedictine monk stationed in Africa was with us, as was a retired German abbot who had been in the army during World War II. The abbot explained to me how tedious it was learning the goosestep. A Filipino Benedictine monk, one from England, another from Australia, and an Irish Cistercian were also along. The Americans in the program were from various areas of the country and had been in monastic life for a number of years. On this trip to Norcia, we were joined by several full-time students at Sant'Anselmo, mostly young monks from all over the world.

We waited in the rain for close to an hour before the bus arrived. Some of us shared umbrellas, but Father Fabian, the English monk among us old-timers, was the only one who was realistically prepared for the weather. He was decked out in waders and a rubber suit. Neither was the bus driver prepared. He was late picking us up because of the congested morning traffic in Rome, and he was angry because he had to drive us to the Sabine Hills, where ice and snow were reported to be covering the roads.

Father Ambrose, an American monk on the faculty at Sant'Anselmo and our guide, urged us onto the bus, warning us not to joke with the driver. Outside of Rome, the rain stopped, but the driver was still in an irritable mood. A young American monk, who was standing in the aisle talking with me, was told to go back to his seat and to stay there. I was wishing that the bus driver could have the opportunity of driving on South Dakota roads in a blizzard. When we arrived in the Sabine Hills, we saw snow, but the roads were clear, and the driver was relieved.

Norcia is located in a valley at the base of Monti Sibillini. It's an old walled town with a statue of its most famous son in the city square. The Basilica of St. Benedict is a few feet from the statue. After a visit to the crypt of the church, where tradition places the births of Benedict and Scholastica, we went upstairs to celebrate Mass. There was no heat in the basilica, and even some of the concelebrating priests wore gloves. We had to remove our gloves, though, to sign the guest book. Only a short time before our visit, Pope John Paul II had signed the book. It was the year the Benedictines and the whole world were celebrating the 1500th anniversary of Benedict and Scholastica's birth on this very site. A more recent tradition locates their birthplace outside of town at what is now a cemetery. We went there too—just to make sure we'd been to the correct site.

City Hall is across the street from the basilica. In 1980, this is where the relic of St. Benedict was kept. It was explained to us that the diocesan cathedral was down the street, and St. Scholastica's relic was housed there. On the Feast of Benedict the relics—his and hers—are carried in two processions that converge in the square. Brother and sister are reunited in the center of their hometown. Although it's believed that the two saints are entombed together at Monte Cassino, parts of them seem to have found their way all around the world.

There were patches of ice on the cobblestone streets, and the rooftops were covered with snow. On our way to lunch at a restaurant run by the Norcian Benedictine nuns, we passed an elderly woman standing in the doorway of her house. She greeted all the monks, and then showed us her bruised elbow. She'd slipped on the ice that morning.

Some of the townspeople were in the *ristorante* when all of us crowded in, leaving room for no one else. The meal was superb. Everything we ate came from the nuns' garden and farm. After the meal, we were served a delicious orange liqueur. We raved about it. Then the abbess served a lemon one that was even better. The nuns had made the liqueur, naturally.

At the time there was a small community of Benedictine monks in Norcia, exiles from Czechoslovakia. We drove past their monastery on the way out of town. The bus driver was in a much better mood after the meal. The Czechs have since moved elsewhere, and American monks live in Norcia now. The principle work of this small monastery is the care of the basilica built over the childhood home of Benedict and Scholastica. Norcia is a charming place, and its citizens are friendly. I can understand why Benedict didn't like living in Rome. I come from a small town myself.

Our group traveled from Norcia to Monte Cassino and Subiaco. The Lombards destroyed Monte Cassino in 590, and the Saracens destroyed it again in 843. An earthquake damaged it in 1349, and Allied bombers made rubble of the monastery in 1944. The monks of Monte Cassino describe this last destruction as "the notorious bombardment of February 15, 1944." When our group visited the Cradle of Western Monasticism, the Americans were cautioned not to reveal our citizenship. If any of the monks at Monte Cassino had not forgiven us for bombing their monastery, even more of them were disturbed by the fact that America takes credit for financing its reconstruction. They insist that it was done "with the financial aid of the Italian government alone." Some of us Americans couldn't understand why the monastery was rebuilt exactly as it was. It seemed impractical to use plans from the seventeenth and eighteenth centuries to construct a monastery in the twentieth. The Germans are a practical people, and have led the way in modern ecclesiastical architecture. I wondered what the German abbot thought about the situation at Monte Cassino.

I tried praying at the tomb of Benedict and his sister, but the lay custodian followed us around the sanctuary and would not let us find any peace. When we sat in the choir stalls, he jangled his keys at us. When we tried entering the sacristy, he screamed at us. We were not wearing monastic habits. If he had heard the Americans speaking, he might have judged that we were just another busload of tourists—a men's organization like the Veterans of Foreign Wars. Some of us looked old enough to have been in the one that left Monte Cassino in ruins for the fourth time in its history.

Subiaco is where Benedict lived in a cave for three years after taking flight from Rome. A monk named Romanus brought him meals, lowering them into the cave in a basket tied to a rope. The Emperor Nero had built himself a palace at Subiaco, and created a lake by damming up a river. On our way up the mountain to the Sacro Speco (Sacred Cave) we passed by the place where Nero's palace once stood.

We were joined on this trip by thirty American priests who were in a renewal program of their own in Rome. They outnumbered the Benedictines, but that didn't matter. The American monks were glad to be joined by people from home. Several of the priests had been educated at schools run by the Benedictines. "Hey, I studied at St. John's in Minnesota," one shouted. Others had been to St. Meinrad's in Indiana, St. Bernard's in Alabama, and St. Gregory's in Oklahoma. I was surprised to see a priest from Minnesota I knew. He later became an oblate of our community.

It was possible to pray in the cave without being disturbed. There was no custodian scolding us as at Monte Cassino. The walls of the buildings constructed over the Sacro Speco are covered with frescoes from the Middle Ages, including the one of a guest named Francis of Assisi. The cave clings to the side of a mountain from which there is a breathtaking view of the wooded Aniene Valley below. Petrarch visited Subiaco in the fourteenth century, and thought he was on the threshold of paradise.

We had brought brown bag lunches to Monte Cassino, but at Subiaco we were given wine and cheese and bread. The guest master was an Australian by birth. He found his way to the Benedictines at Subiaco years ago and joined them. I wonder if St. Benedict ever had any regrets about leaving. After our little repast at the cave, we went into town for lunch—a five-course meal—at the end of which, and after having drunk several glasses of wine, the Americans felt like singing. Back in Rome when the American priests had boarded the bus, making as much noise as prep school boys on an outing, I'd overheard the German in our group whisper to the Swiss, "Ja, Americans." Now, after their having had several glasses of wine, the German and Swiss were able to comprehend Americans and, surprisingly enough, they were able to join in the singing of some of our songs. Even our Italian waiter knew "Deep in the Heart of Texas." The medley ended when the waiter shouted, "Shut up!" good-naturedly. It was time to clean the tables. The siesta hour was approaching. We went back to Rome and dropped off the diocesan priests at their house of studies. "So long," they said. "See you in the States." The alumni of our schools said, "It was good being with the Bennies again."

What is so significant about Subiaco? It is the place where Benedict found his vocation. He tried living there in solitude, but it became apparent that he was not suited to the life of a hermit. Shepherds discovered him and sought his advice. It was here that he learned the disadvantage of being a solitary. On Easter day, a priest from nearby came to the cave and advised Benedict that he shouldn't be fasting on such a great feast. Benedict had become too much out of touch. In the Rule he would write that a monk might become a hermit only after he has been tempered by life in community. Benedict was called from the cave by the monks at Vicovaro, a town we passed on our way to Subiaco.

The abbot had died and the monks were looking for another one who would tolerate their wayward manner of living. When Benedict tried reforming them, they attempted to kill him by poisoning his wine. He returned to Subiaco and set about organizing monastic life as he saw fit. Later, he moved to Monte Cassino where he wrote the Holy Rule, and died. What would have happened if Benedict had left his talent hidden under a bushel basket, if he had stayed in the cave the rest of his life?

Dorothy Day: A Fellow Benedictine

I had never heard of Dorothy Day until an autumn evening in 1954 when a classmate at St. John's University invited me to accompany him to a home off campus, where she was going to speak about the Catholic Worker Movement. Although Day was fifty-seven years of age in 1954, I thought she looked much older. Her hair was gray, and the braid circling her head made her look old-fashioned. She wore no makeup. Her dress appeared to be a hand-me-down. She had a grandmotherly appearance and demeanor. I couldn't understand why Paul had told me she was a radical. When she spoke, I understood why. Dorothy Day was as radical as the Gospel of Jesus Christ.

She was a single parent and a freelance journalist who met Peter Maurin, a Christian anarchist, in 1933. The Catholic Worker Movement began in New York City when they started a soup line and opened a house of hospitality for victims of the Great Depression. They also began publishing a paper. After Maurin's death, Day remained steadfast in her service to the poor and the oppressed. Of course she was misunderstood and even maligned. I knew a priest who invited her to breakfast in the rectory after seeing her in church one morning. The pastor told him not to bring that "riff-raff" into the house. This was in the same town where, as a college student, I had heard her speak.

No doubt some ecclesiastics found her too difficult to take. In an interview with Robert Coles in the early 1970s, she said,

"When I see the church siding with the powerful and forgetting the weak, and when I see bishops living in luxury and the poor being ignored or thrown crumbs, I know that Jesus is being insulted . . . The church doesn't belong to officials and bureaucrats. It belongs to all its people, and especially its most humble men and women and children."

Before her conversion to Catholicism in 1928, Day was a friend of Jack Reed, who was a Harvard graduate, a socialist writer for a New York magazine called *The Masses,* and was portrayed in the movie *Reds.* Dorothy worked on the staff of *The Masses,* and she knew other idealists, reformers, and radicals from that time. One of them, playwright Eugene O'Neill, introduced her to Francis Thompson's "The Hound of Heaven." She recalled in her autobiography, *The Long Loneliness,* that he often read the poem in a saloon called Hell Hole by its patrons. "The recurrence of it, the inevitableness of the outcome made me feel that sooner or later I would have to pause in the mad rush of living and remember my first beginning and my last end." She had been raised in a family that was nominally Christian, but she had turned away from organized religion in college. The initial price she paid for becoming a Catholic was costly. The relationship with the man she loved, and who was the father of her child, had to come to an end. He would not marry her nor reconcile himself to the fact that she had found religion.

In 1955, Dorothy became an oblate of St. Procopius Abbey in Lisle, Illinois. In her lifetime, she manifested so many Benedictine virtues and values. Hospitality, of course, is the first thing that comes to mind. She lived in poverty among the poor in whom St. Benedict said Christ is more specifically received. Stanley Vishnewski, who went to help out at the Catholic Worker in 1934 at the age of seventeen, and stayed for the remainder of his life, wrote years later: "The Benedictine tradition has had a great influence on the Catholic Worker Movement. The truth expressed by St. Benedict that work is prayer has been one of the animating ideas in developing a philosophy of labor. The Benedictine spirit of the recitation of the Divine Office has influenced the Catholic Worker prayer life. Take away St. Benedict's ideas of hospitality, guesthouses, farming communes, liturgical prayer, and there is very little left in the Catholic Worker program."

When Dorothy died in 1980, Kenneth L. Woodward wrote in *Newsweek* that for nearly half a century, "Dorothy Day was the radical heart and conscience of American Catholicism. She took the Sermon on the Mount as a practical guide for life, not as a pious ideal. She was a pacifist who went the extra mile, protesting air-raid shelters as well as nuclear armaments. She was a social anarchist who refused to pay taxes or accept institutional support, insisting that the only true charity is personal service to the poor. To be alive, she believed, was to be 'On Pilgrimage'—which was the title of the column she wrote in *The Catholic Worker,* her penny-a-copy tabloid that hasn't changed its price, type or editorial stance in 47 years."

Dorothy Day came to Blue Cloud Abbey in the spring of 1971, when she was seventy-four years old. She had difficulty walking because of the rheumatism in her knees, but she had taken the bus from New York City to South Dakota for talks at two colleges in our state. At one of them, she had been put on a panel with feminists, which perturbed her. I wanted to suggest that she was a model for them. Dorothy had been in jail many times, but her first confinement was in 1917 when she was arrested with suffragists outside the White House. She had other complaints as well: priests and religious who didn't wear identifiable garb and certain aberrations in the liturgy. Not only did she look like a grandmother, she sounded like any number of them who couldn't abide such changes in the 1970s.

We had silver rosaries from Guatemala for sale in our shop, and she admired them. I gave her one, and she promised to pray the first ten decades for me. "The rosary is such a comfort to have with me on a picket line," she said. Ah, Dorothy, I thought, you haven't given up.

Feeding the hungry, sheltering the homeless, clothing the naked—these things cannot be criticized. During World War II, many Catholic Workers themselves found fault with her pacifism, and departed from the movement because they could not adhere to this teaching. In 1941 she wrote, "We wish the workers would lay down their tools and refuse to make the instruments of death. We wish that they were so convinced of the immorality of modern wars that they would refuse to make the instruments of those wars." In 1965, she and other women fasted for ten days and prayed while the Fathers of the Vatican Council debated an official teaching on modern warfare. They did condemn the use of nuclear weapons. During the Vietnam era, Dorothy had an even more personal reason for protesting war. She had a grandson in that conflict.

Although Dorothy Day did not live in a monastery, she belonged to a community and knew both the joys and frustrations of communal life. Among the people who find shelter at the Catholic Worker, some need what St. Benedict calls "supporting with the greatest patience one another's weaknesses of body or behavior" (*RB* 72.5). It was sometimes predicted that the Catholic Worker Movement would die with Dorothy, but it didn't. No doubt the Catholic Worker and the Benedictines have both survived because of the principles they share. Today there are 130 Catholic Worker communities in thirty-two states and eight foreign countries.

Some people called Dorothy Day a living saint. Dorothy resented this. "I will not be so easily dismissed," she retorted whenever reference was made to her sanctity. This is something Benedict cautions against too. "Do not aspire to be called holy before you really are, but first be holy that you may truly be called so" (*RB* 4.62). Before leaving Blue Cloud Abbey that day in 1971, I asked her to sign one of the books she had authored. She wrote: "With grateful affection from a fellow Benedictine. Dorothy Day."

Around the World

Fewer men and women are entering monasteries in Europe and North America, but there is an increase of new members in Latin America, Africa, and Asia. Europeans founded a number of these communities in the nineteenth century. Their growth and success were nourished by the martyrdom of both men and women members in the foreign missions.

Many other monasteries came into existence in the following century. Our community established Resurrection Priory in Guatemala forty years ago. There are only three gringo monks in the community now. Membership continues to grow with vocations from Guatemala and other Central American countries. In time Resurrection Priory will become independent from us just as we became independent from our mother abbey.

Padre Carlos, a Guatemalan, spent the year 2004 with us. While here in South Dakota he found a ministry among the many Hispanic people who have come to the States for the sake of employment, many of whom work at the large dairies near us. Just as Benedictines left Germany and Switzerland to minister to German-speaking immigrants in the United States, now is a time when Spanish-speaking Benedictines have an opportunity to care for the Latino population, even in places as far north as South Dakota.

The Benedictine sisters of Erie, Pennsylvania, staff the office for The Alliance of International Monasticism (AIM). This organization raises funds and provides material resources for Benedictine and Cistercian monasteries. American Benedictine women have themselves gone to Africa to offer workshops in spirituality and human development. One year AIM USA procured printing equipment for a community of Benedictine Sisters in Brazil, library books for a school run by monks in Ho Chi Minh City, Vietnam, and the high school tuition for Benedictine sisters in Tanzania.

When a fire totally destroyed three of the five buildings at the Abbey of the Immaculate Heart of Mary at Vigan in The Philippines, AIM came to the assistance of the sisters. Lost in the fire were the novitiate quarters and classrooms, the library, chapter room, and church. Faulty, fifty-year-old electrical wiring was to blame for the fire. Four sewing machines burned up, and a piano and organ as well as all the other musical instruments. The Divine Office books, hymnals, and missals were all reduced to ashes. The nuns had not been the only ones to use the church; the people of the neighborhood also worshiped there.

The Benedictine nuns of Vigan are enclosed, but they have outreach programs that benefit people around them. A choir of sixty children from among the poor sang at the liturgies and elsewhere. The poor and elderly received special care at the monastery, and people seeking a place for solitude and reflection were always welcome.

In a letter describing the devastation, the abbess asked for help rebuilding the chapel and reestablishing the library. True to their Benedictine calling, with the season of Lent approaching, she cited St. Benedict's Rule: "During this time of Lent each one is to receive a book from the library, and is to read the whole of it straight through" (*RB* 48.15). Mother Celeste said she would be happy to have some books to give the sisters before Ash Wednesday.

St. Benedict Speaks

On the day Benedict died, two monks had a vision of a road leading from Monte Cassino up into the heavens. An angel asked if they knew who had taken that road. They didn't, and the angel told them St. Benedict had taken this road on his way to heaven. The road used by Benedict is the one we're traveling right now. He has given us a map for our journey. The Rule is our travel guide. He has pointed out some of the dangers we should avoid along the way. If we take a wrong turn, he urges us to get back on the right road.

First of all, he tells us that on this journey we should serve one another in love. Your service is recognized, he says, but don't crave praise. Don't hold your fellow travelers captive by your talents. Take pride in your work, but do not become proud yourselves. Do not live entirely off the labors of others. Look how Cluny got out of hand, and a lot of other places, too. Haven't I urged you to live by the labor of your own hands? Please do not become a burden to society.

Don't ever let work become an excuse, however, to forsake prayer. Don't become so absorbed in one thing that you forget the others. Ours is a life of balance and moderation. If neither prayer nor work seems appealing, you are probably bored. Shake off this boredom, this lethargy.

Are you really convinced that the tasks asked of you are beyond your capabilities? Do not hesitate to try new works. Attempt something first, and then come back to me if things aren't working out. Remember how Aelred protested when he was asked to write a little book on charity in the monastic life? It has become a classic, but Bernard had to convince him that he had the ability to write. You, too, should encourage one another.

Monastic people have achieved great works because of their efforts. You built Mont St. Michel. The first poet of the English language heard his calling in a monastery. Roswitha, one of my nuns, although a medieval playwright, is sometimes called the "Mother of Modern Drama." Creative works have remained a fixed tradition in our monasteries.

Nor have my followers scorned learning—the kind I fled from in my youth. My school of the Lord's service has educated millions of young people. It has produced numerous brilliant teachers and scholars: Bede, Anselm, Jean Mabillon, to mention but three. Of course you did let Thomas Aquinas get away from you at Monte Cassino. But you are to be commended for expelling young Adolph Hitler from the school at Feicht. Maybe, though, if you'd worked harder with that incorrigible youth, things would have turned out differently. Among my followers there have been so many women of intellectual renown: the nuns Gertrud, Mechtild, Hildegard; and the oblate, Elena Lucrezia Cornaro Piscopia, the first woman in Europe to earn a Ph.D. She would have preferred studying theology, but women were not allowed to do this in the seventeenth century.

Oh yes, you've been imparters of knowledge, but not just in schools. Knowledge is also imparted in sermons, in conversations. Knowledge, of course, comes from books, and oh, how you've valued your books. When Monte Cassino was sacked, you fled with your library books and left behind my bones and those of my sister.

You have carried our Lord's gospel to various parts of the world, and some of my monks are known as the Apostles of certain areas of the world: Augustine in England, Boniface in Germany, Willibrord in the Low Countries, Rupert in Austria, Adalbert in Bohemia and Poland, and Ansgar in Scandinavia.

Throughout history you have taught people how to pray. In more recent times, three of my monks, Virgil Michel, Godfrey Diekmann, and the Anglican Gregory Dix, developed in the faithful an appreciation for liturgical prayer.

You have served humanity well. Taking to heart my words regarding the sick, you have shown them Christ-like concern in your many hospitals. Frances of Rome cared for the indigent and the ill in the fourteenth century. Another oblate, Dorothy Day, dedicated her life to the poor and the promotion of social justice in the twentieth century. You have come to the rescue of people who were shunned—the deaf, for example. They were excluded from society before a Spanish monk of mine taught them sign language. Is there anyone treated that way in your day? It pleases me that you never turn away from anyone who needs your love. You know everyone was always welcomed at my monastery as Christ himself.

My followers are increasingly known for dialoguing with people of other religious traditions. In the twentieth century the Belgian monk Lambert Beauduin was the Apostle of Ecumenism. He was the friend of the Orthodox and other Christians. And now in the twenty-first century my monks and nuns are dialoguing with their counterparts among the Buddhists and other groups throughout the world.

Do not belittle yourselves, thinking monks and nuns are useless citizens, people of no consequences. Are you North Americans and Europeans worried about numbers? You needn't have a lot of members in order to live a decent monastic life. When it all began, we were only a few men who took up housekeeping together and the praise of God in common. I wasn't accompanied by many monks when we went from Subiaco to found Monte Cassino. It never occurred to me that the place would become known as the "Cradle of Western Monasticism." Nor did I have the slightest inkling that historians would call these followers of my way of life the saviors of civilization.

Continue practicing the good zeal I describe in my Rule. And recall my words: "Let them prefer nothing whatever to

Christ, and may he bring us all together to everlasting life" (*RB* 72.11-12).

These words of St. Benedict at the close of chapter 72 of The Rule made Abbot St. Odo of Cluny believe that when all of us motley monastics have reached the destination at the end of the road, Benedict will be so happy to see us that he'll dance for joy. And Benedict dancing with our motley crew is one of my favorite images of heaven.

Sources

Aelred of Rievaulx. *The Mirror of Charity*, trans. by Elizabeth Connor, O.C.S.O. Kalamazoo, MI: Cistercian Publications, 1990.

Alcoholics Anonymous. New York: Alcoholics Anonymous World Services, Inc., Fourth Edition, 2001.

Anguillaria, Mary Magdalene. *The Life of Saint Francis of Rome*. New York: Catholic Book Publishing Company, The Liturgy of the Hours, Vol. II, 1975.

Anson, Peter F. *Abbot Extraordinary*. New York: Sheed and Ward, 1958.

Bede. *A History of the English Church and People*, trans. by Leo Sherley-Price, revised by R. E. Latham. New York: Penguin Viking, 1968.

Coles, Robert. *Dorothy Day: A Radical Devotion*. Reading, MS: Addison-Wesley Publishing, 1987.

Daly, Lowrie J., S.J. *Benedictine Monasticism: Its Formation and Development Through the 12th Century*. New York: Sheed and Ward, 1965.

Day, Dorothy. *The Catholic Worker*, April 1941.

Day, Dorothy. *The Long Loneliness*. New York: Harper and Brothers, 1952.

Farmer, D. H., ed. *The Age of Bede*. New York: Penguin Viking, 1983.

Gregory the Great, St. *Homilies on Ezekiel*. New York: Catholic Book Publishing Company, The Liturgy of the Hours, Vol. IV, 1975.

Hilpisch, Stephanus, O.S.B. *History of Benedictine Nuns,* trans. by Sister Joanne Muggli, O.S.B. Collegeville, MN: St. John's Abbey Press, 1958.

Hume, Basil, O.S.B. *Searching for God.* Petersham, MA: St. Bede's Publications, 1977.

Kardong, Terrence G., O.S.B. *Benedict's Rule: A Translation and Commentary.* Collegeville, MN: Liturgical Press, 1996.

Kessler, Ann, O.S.B. *Benedictine Men and Women of Courage: Roots and History.* Yankton, SD: Sacred Heart Monastery, 1996.

Knowles, David. *Saints and Scholars.* New York: Cambridge University Press, 1962.

Mohler, James, S.J. *The Heresy of Monasticism.* Staten Island, NY: Alba House, 1971.

Newman, John Henry Cardinal. *Historical Sketches: Vol. II.* Westminster, MD: Christian Classics, Inc., 1970.

Rippinger, Joel, O.S.B. *The Benedictine Order in the United States: An Interpretive History.* Collegeville, MN: Liturgical Press, 1990.

Schmitt, Miriam, O.S.B., and Linda Kulzer, O.S.B. *Medieval Women Monastics: Wisdom's Wellsprings.* Collegeville, MN: Liturgical Press, 1996.

Stephen of Lexington. *Letters from Ireland: 1228–1229,* trans., intro. by Barry W. O'Dwyer. Kalamazoo, MI: Cistercian Publications, 1982.

Nichols, John A., and Lillian Thomas Shank, eds. *Distant Echoes: Medieval Religious Women, Vol. One.* Kalamazoo, MI: Cistercian Publications, 1984.

Prescott, H.F.M. *The Man on a Donkey.* New York: Macmillian, 1952.

Sutera, Judith, O.S.B. *True Daughters: Monastic Identity and American Benedictine Women's History.* Atchison, KS: Benedictine College Press, 1987.

Talbot, C. H., trans. and ed. *The Anglo-Saxon Missionaries in Germany*. New York: Sheed and Ward, 1954.

Van Zeller, Hubert, O.S.B. *The Benedictine Idea*. London: Burns and Oates, 1959.

Woodward, Kenneth L. "The End of a Pilgrimage," *Newsweek*, December 15, 1980.

The text of the Rule is from *RB 1980: the Rule of St. Benedict in English*, ed. Timothy Fry, O.S.B., 1981. The quotes from the second book of *Dialogues* of St. Gregory the Great are from *Life and Miracles of Saint Benedict*, trans. Odo J. Zimmerman, O.S.B., and Benedict R. Avery, O.S.B., 1949. Both are published by Liturgical Press, Collegeville, MN.

Although I am not a monastic historian by training, I have taught Benedictine history to our novices for a number of years. It has been one of my pleasures in life. Much of the material for this Benedictine history in a nutshell was assembled from my class notes during another one of those years when we had no novices.

Brother Benet Tvedten, O.S.B.